C000003693

SPANISH-ENGLISH
GRAMMAR
Pocket Dictionary

**600 KEY TERMS FULLY AND CLEARLY
DEFINED WITH EXEMPLARY SENTENCES**

**SPECIALLY DEVELOPED FOR
U.S. HIGH SCHOOL AND
COLLEGE STUDENTS OF SPANISH**

CARLOS B. VEGA, Ph.D.

BARRON'S

Carlos B. Vega is a graduate of Indiana University and the University of Madrid, and author of over 40 books on language, literature, and history. He has taught Spanish for over 30 years at several U.S. colleges and universities.

All inquiries should be addressed to:
Barron's Educational Series, Inc.
250 Wireless Boulevard
Hauppauge, NY 11788
www.barronseduc.com

ISBN-13: 978-0-7641-4533-9
ISBN-10: 0-7641-4533-9

Library of Congress Control Number 2009045516

Library of Congress Cataloging-in-Publication Data
Vega, Carlos B.
   Spanish-English grammar pocket dictionary : 600 key terms
   fully and clearly explained with examples / Carlos B. Vega.
      p. cm.
   Includes bibliographical references and index.
   ISBN-13: 978-0-7641-4533-9 (alk. paper)
   ISBN-10: 0-7641-4533-9 (alk. paper)
   1. Spanish language—Dictionaries.—English.   2. English
   language—Dictionaries—Spanish   I. Title.

PC4640.S5967 2009
463'.21—dc22   2009045516

Printed in China
9 8 7 6 5 4 3 2 1

CONTENTS

INTRODUCTION

Students have to struggle constantly with a multitude of grammatical terms that impede their understanding and learning of Spanish, and, although there are several Spanish grammar dictionaries available today, they are intended primarily for the scholar and specialist and provide little or no examples. Additionally, most of them are dated and geared exclusively to a Spanish-speaking audience.

In view of the above, we have developed this new dictionary hoping that it would serve the student well. It provides a selection of over 600 key terms clearly and succinctly explained with an abundance of examples in both English and Spanish. It is specifically geared to U.S. students of Spanish at the junior-senior secondary and undergraduate college levels. In addition, it could prove valuable to graduate students and professionals in general and also as a good review of Spanish grammar. Although comprehensive, it is not an all-inclusive grammatical lexicon, nor does it include linguistic or literary terms. All explanations are given in English, with examples provided both in Spanish and English.

If you need to get more information about a Spanish word, you may consult any of the specialized works listed in the bibliography, or visit the website of the

Royal Spanish Academy of the Language in Madrid at *www.rae.es/rae.html*. Write in the word you want and you will get an immediate definition. For a comprehensive listing of Spanish words, the best sources are the *Diccionario de uso del español,* by María Moliner, and *Enciclopedia del idioma,* by Martín Alonso. For linguistic terms, the best source is the *Diccionario de términos filológicos,* by Fernando Lázaro Carreter (all are listed in the bibliography). Another good source is the *Diccionario gramatical,* by Emilio M. Martínez Amador. Bear in mind, however, that all of these books are quite scholarly and require dedicated reading and study. For Spanish grammar, we would recommend the *Gramática esencial de la lengua española de Manuel Seco,* by Manuel Seco, and for Spanish Phonetics, the *Manual de pronunciación española,* by Navarro Tomás (also in the bibliography). To purchase any of these books at reasonable prices, we recommend *www.abebooks.com* the website of *Abebooks.* The first—and still claimed to be the best—Spanish grammar is *Gramática de la lengua castellana,* by Antonio de Nebrija (1441–1522), published in Madrid in 1492, and also his other three books, *Latin-Spanish* (1492), *Spanish-Latin* (1495), and *Reglas de ortografía española* (Rules of Spanish Orthography, 1495). In the same esteemed category as Nebrija is Andrés Bello (Caracas, Venezuela, 1781–1865), whose *Gramática de la lengua castellana* (1847), remains a classic. Other useful books are *Vocabulario de Cervantes,* by Carlos Fernández Gómez (Real Academia Española, Madrid, 1962), and, by don Ramón Menéndez Pidal (1869–1968), *Orígenes del español* (1926) and *Manual de gramática histórica* (1904).

All entries are listed first in Spanish and then in English, using the following abbreviations for each:

m/f	(masculine or feminine) for all nouns, **pl** for the plural.
adj	adjective
adv	adverb
conj	conjunction
prep	preposition
pron	pronoun
v	verb

We feel that this dictionary was greatly needed and long overdue, and that it should be considered the first of its kind. We are confident that students of Spanish everywhere will find it very useful and practical.

The author

abecé – m / *ABCs* The alphabet.

a personal – f / *personal a* Always used in Spanish before direct objects or pronouns referring to persons, as in: Veo a Matilde. (I see Matilde.); La veo a ella. (I see her.)

abecedario – m / *alphabet* The Spanish alphabet is composed of 29 letters with 5 vowels and 24 consonants. Note that the *w* is only used in the writing of foreign names, principally English and German. In many of these names the *w* has been transcribed as *v* in Spanish, as in: wagon > vagón, but remains *w* in the writing of foreign proper names, as in: Washington, Wagner. Its name is "uve doble," "ve doble," or "doble v."

The Spanish Alphabet:

A B C CH D E F G H I J K L LL M N Ñ O P Q R S T U V W X Y Z

The letters *CH, LL, RR* count as one letter and can't be divided, as in: no-che, ca-ba-llo, ca-rro. In the first two, only the first letter is capitalized: *Ch, Ll.* The *H* in Spanish is always silent (mute) in pronunciation.

abreviatura – f / *abbreviation* Some examples in Spanish are: gral. (general), pág. (página), Ud. (usted). Generally, they are not used as frequently in Spanish as they are in English.

absorción – f / *absorption* The disappearance of a vowel when incorporated to a neighboring consonantal sound.

accidente gramatical – m / *grammatical accident* Something belonging to a word but not necessarily being part of it, like gender, number, person, or tense. Basically, it is an inflected modification of a variable word expressing a grammatical category. Examples: Leticia y Margarita estudian. (Leticia and Margaret study.); La nieve es blanca. (The snow is white.) The inflected words are "estudian" and "blanca."

acento – m / *accent* The stressed syllable in the pronunciation of a word, distinguishing it from the rest of the syllables by its intonation or tone.

acento de grupo – m / *group accent* (See: proclítica, palabra)

acento de intensidad – m / *stress accent* The stress distinguishing a syllable when it is stressed more than the others, as in: caramelo (candy) > ca-ra-ME-lo. It can have or have not a written accent mark.

acento diacrítico – m / *diacritical accent* It is used to differentiate the meaning of homonymous words. Examples: te (pronoun), té (tea), si (conjunction, if), sí (adverb, yes).

acento ortográfico – m / *orthographic/written accent* There is only one written or orthographical accent in Spanish, which is essential in the pronunciation and writing of words that don't conform to the accentuation rules. In fact, without it, thousands of Spanish words would be mispronounced and hard to understand. This accent is used both in lower and upper case letters. Examples with all the vowels are:

lower case	upper case
árbol	Árbol
éxito	Éxito
ímpetu	Ímpetu
óleo	Óleo
único	Único

Examples of mispronunciation by the omission of the written accent are:

without the accent	with the accent
oido	oído
the stress would go on the last syllable *(do)*	
fisica	física
the stress would go on the second syllable *(si)*	
accion	acción
the stress would go on the first syllable *(ac)*	
ademas	además
the stress would go on the second syllable *(de)*	
celebre	célebre
the stress would go on the second syllable *(le)*	

acento prosódico – m / *prosodic accent* The stressed syllable in the pronunciation of a word. Except for monosyllabic words, all words in Spanish have a syllable that is pronounced with higher intensity than the others. Examples: hambre (HAM-bre), cuaderno (cua-DER-no), perro (PE-rro). The prosodic accent doesn't have a written accent, and includes words (the vast majority) that follow rule #1 and rule #2 of Spanish accentuation. Rule #1: Words ending in a vowel or *n* or *s* are stressed on the next to the last syllable. Rule #2: Words ending in a consonant other than *n* or *s* are stressed on the last syllable.

acentuación – f / *accentuation* The pronunciation of a word by intensifying the prosodic accent or by placing a written accent on the intensified syllable. Examples: caramelo (caraMElo, the *ME* is the prosodic accent), árbol (AR-bol, the first syllable is intensified by the written accent). The rules of accentuation in Spanish are:

1. If a word ends in a vowel, *n*, or *s*, the stress would fall on the next to the last syllable, as in: CAsa, LIbro.

2. If a word ends in a consonant other than *n* or *s*, the stress would fall on the last syllable, as in: capiTAL, caLOR.

3. If any word doesn't follow rule 1 or 2, it must carry a written accent mark over the stressed syllable, as in: hábito, armónico.

The classification of words according to the accent are:

Palabras llanas/graves: the stress falls on the next to the last syllable.

Palabras agudas: the stress falls on the last syllable.

Palabras esdrújulas: the stress falls on the second from the last syllable.

Palabras sobresdrújulas: the stress falls on the third from the last syllable.

"Esdrújula" and "sobresdrújula" words must carry a written accent mark, as in:

esdrújula	carácter
sobresdrújula	Devuélvemelo.

In Spanish, there are no "sobresdrújula" words per se, but only those formed by adding two unaccented pronouns to the verb preceding them, as in: Cántamelo. (Sing it for me.); Cómpraselo. (Buy it for him/her.) The written accent is also used in adjectives linked by a dash, whether they are two or more, as in: manual teórico-práctico, or tratado biográfico-histórico-crítico. Exceptions (not separated by a dash) are the "gentilicios" (name given to the people of a particular country or region), for example: hispanoamericano, indoeuropeo. The conjunction "o" must carry a written accent when it is written between numbers, like: 10 ó 20. A written accent mark *may* be placed over foreign names to conform to Spanish pronunciation: Wáshington, Jéfferson, Mózart.

acepción – f / *meaning* The meaning or sense of a word as per its context.

adagio – m / *adage* A brief saying or maxim, often moralistic in nature and in metaphoric form, like: Del lobo un pelo. (Get what you can.); No pongas todos los huevos en una canasta. (Don't put all your eggs in one basket.)

adjetivo – m/ *adjective* A word used with a noun to modify it, limit it, define it, specify it, or describe it. Examples: El hombre es perezoso. (The man is lazy.); Mi padre es alto. (My father is tall.); Las casas son viejas. (The houses are old.) There are different kinds of adjectives (see the various entries under "adjetivo"). If the adjective refers to various nouns with different genders, the masculine form is always used. Example: Las casas y los apartamentos están hoy muy caros. (The houses and apartments are today very expensive.) The adjective corresponding to two or more nouns will always be used in the plural, even if the nouns are in the singular. Example: Al llegar a casa vi la puerta y la ventana abiertas. (Upon getting home, I saw the door and the window open.)

adjetivo aumentativo – m / *augmentative adjective* Augmentative and diminutive adjectives suggest the increase or decrease of things or the intensity or toning down of their qualities. Often, however, they are also used to indicate a feeling of contempt, scorn, or esteem independent from any idea of size. They are formed by adding various suffixes to nouns or adjectives. Here are a few examples:

augmentative (size)

-ón/ona	muchachón/muchachona	big guy/big gal
-azo/aza	perrazo/bocaza	big dog/big mouth
-ote/ota	hombrote/mujerota	big man/big woman

diminutive

-ito/ita	pequeñito/botellita	tiny/tiny bottle
-illo/illa	pajarillo/florecilla	tiny bird/flower
-ico/ica	buenico/inteligentica	goodhearted/somewhat intelligent

pejorative

-aco	libraco	bad book
-acho	poblacho	shantytown
-ucho	medicucho	quack
-uela	mujerzuela	bad woman (slut)
-uza	gentuza	riffraff/rabble

adjetivo calificativo – m / *qualifying adjective*

Denotes a quality of the noun it modifies, as in: Juan es muy inteligente. (John is very intelligent.); Mis padres son muy simpáticos. (My parents are very nice.) Some qualifying adjectives have different meanings depending on whether they precede or follow the noun. For example, it is not the same to say "un pobre hombre" than "un hombre pobre," just as in English there is a difference between these two phrases:

That man is poor.   (He doesn't have money.)
Poor man!   (One having many problems.)

In the majority of cases, however, it makes no difference whether the qualifying adjective is used before or after the noun; for example, whether we say "una noche preciosa" or "una preciosa noche" (a beautiful night). In English, however, the adjective generally precedes the noun and in Spanish it follows it: the red house (la casa roja).

adjetivo comparativo – m / *comparative adjective* Denotes a comparison that can be of superiority, inferiority (or inequality), or equality. In Spanish it uses the following forms:

Spanish	English
superiority: más… que	more… than
inferiority: menos… que	less… than
equality: tan… como	as… as

It is used with nouns, adjectives, or adverbs.
Examples:

superiority

Mi hermana es más alta que la tuya.	My sister is taller than yours.

inferiority

Tu hermana es menos alta que la mía.	Your sister is shorter than mine.

Here, we could also say "Tu hermana es más baja que la mía." (Which could also mean in English "Your sister is shorter than mine.")

equality

Tu hermana es tan alta como la mía.	Your sister is as tall as mine.

The following adjectives have irregular forms in Spanish:

bueno (good)	mejor
malo (bad)	peor
grande (big)	mayor
pequeño (small)	menor

However, in the case of "grande" and "pequeño" when they refer to size, the regular forms are always used, as "mayor" and "menor" are used when they refer to age. Examples:

Mi hermana es mayor que tú.	My sister is older than you.
Tú eres menor que mi hermana.	You are younger than my sister.

adjetivo demostrativo – m / *demonstrative adjective* A demonstrative adjective always precedes the noun and agrees in gender and in number:

Spanish	**English**
este/esta/esto	this
ese/esa/eso	that
aquel/aquella/aquello	that (over there)
estos/estas	these
esos/esas	those
aquellos/aquellas	those (over there)

Examples:

Este carro es rojo.	This car is red.
Esto no me gusta. (neuter)	I don't like this.
Aquellas blusas son preciosas.	Those blouses (over there) are beautiful.

Esos niños son buenos.   Those children are good.

(See important note in: pronombre demostrativo)

adjetivo determinativo – m / *determinative adjective* Determines or specifies the extension of the meaning of the noun. Some of the determinative adjectives in Spanish are: alguno (some), ninguno (none), cierto (certain), otro (another), todo (all), mucho (a lot of), poco (little), mismo (same), ambos (both), cada (each), bastante (enough), demasiado (too much/too many).

adjetivo diminutivo – m / *diminutive adjective* (See: adjetivo aumentativo)

adjetivo gentilicio – m / *gentilitious adjective* Denotes the place of origin or nationality of a person: alemán (German), chino (Chinese), mexicano (Mexican).

adjetivo invariable – m / *invariable adjective* This adjective doesn't change, having the same form in the singular/plural/masculine/feminine. Example: cascarrabias (grumpy): Ese hombre es un cascarrabias. (That man is grumpy.); Esa mujer es una cascarrabias. (That woman is grumpy.); Ese hombre y esa mujer son unos cascarrabias. (That man and that woman are grumpy.)

adjetivo ordinal – m / *ordinal adjective* The one expressing order or succession. Example: primero, segundo, tercero, etc. (first, second, third, etc.).

adjetivo posesivo – m / *possessive adjective*
Denotes possession.

Spanish	English
mi/mis	my
tu/tus	your
su/sus	his/her/its/your (formal)
nuestro/a/os/as	our
vuestro/a/os/as	your (familiar)
su/sus	their/your (formal)

Note: Since "su" and "sus" don't specify the person, the following forms may be added for clarification: de él, de ella, de usted, de ellos, de ellas, de ustedes. Example: Este es su lápiz. Este lápiz es de él. In English they both mean "This is his pencil."

adjetivo predicativo – m / *predicative adjective*
This is the adjective that agrees in gender and number with the subject.

Example:

Los niños han llegado cansados.	The children have arrived tired.

adjetivo superlativo – m / *superlative adjective*
This adjective is expressed in Spanish by the following construction:

> definite article (el, la, los, las) + noun + más or menos + adjective + de

Examples:

¿Quién es más inteligente, tú o José?	Who is more intelligent, you or Joseph?

| José es el más inteligente de los dos. | Joseph is the most intelligent of the two. |

Note: In English, "de" can be either "of" or "in." As with the comparative adjectives, the following superlative adjectives also have irregular forms that are always preceded by the definite articles in both the singular and the plural:

bueno (good) > el/la/los/las mejor/mejores
malo (bad) > el/la/los/las peor/peores
grande (big) > el/la/los/las mayor/mayores
pequeño (small) > el/la/los/las menor/menores

When "grande" and "pequeño" refer to age, "mayor" and "menor" are always used. Examples:

| Tu padre es el mayor. | Your father is the oldest. |
| Tu madre es la menor. | Your mother is the youngest. |

When the noun possesses a higher degree of quality and is not being compared to another, "muy" may be used before the adjective, or the suffix *-ísimo-a-os-as* can be added to the adjective, as follows:

| Juan es muy inteligente. | John is very intelligent. |
| Juan es inteligentísimo. | John is very intelligent. |

Notice that in both cases in English it means "very."

adjunto – adj / *adjunct* Same as "adyacente" (see).

adonde-a donde – adv / *where/to which* This adverb is written as one word when an antecedent is expressed, as in: Te veo en el mismo lugar adonde nos vemos todos los días. (I'll see you in the same place where we see each other every day.) It is written in two words when the antecedent is not expressed, as in: Vamos a donde todos los meses. (We'll go where we go every month.)

adstrato – m / *adstrate/adstratum* A language that exerts influence over another and with which it might share the same geographical area. For example, Spanish and Catalan in Spain, English and French in Canada.

adverbio – m/ *adverb* An adverb is a word that modifies a verb, adjective, or other adverbs. Many adverbs in English are formed by adding the suffix *-ly* to the adjective, as in: slow > slowly, quick > quickly. In Spanish, it is done in the same way by adding the suffix *-mente* to the adjective, as in: alegre > alegremente, general > generalmente. However, if the adjective ends in *o*, it must be changed to *a* before adding *-mente*, as in: claro > claramente. When two adverbs ending in *-mente* are used together, only the second one will have a *-mente* ending. Example: Nos habló clara y sucintamente. (He talked to us clearly and succinctly.) Adjectives having a written accent mark keep it when adding *-mente* to form an adverb. Example: rápido (adjective) > rápidamente (adverb), fácil (adjective) > fácilmente (adverb).

adverbio comparativo – m / *comparative adverb* This adverb denotes comparison. Example:

Josefina baila mejor que tú. (Josephine dances better than you do.) Here, "mejor" is an adverb, not an adjective.

adverbio conjuntivo – m / *conjunctive adverb*
The conjunctive adverb functions as a conjunction, for example: ahora que (now that), aun cuando (even when), bien (well), etc. It forms the so-called "locuciones conjuntivas" (conjunctive phrases). Example in a sentence: Voy contigo ahora que me lo has pedido. (I'll go with you now that you have asked me.)

adverbio correlativo – m / *correlative adverb*
Used with another adverb. It can be: interrogativo (interrogative), demostrativo (demonstrative), relativo (relative). It is interrogative if it is used to ask a question: ¿dónde? (where?), ¿cuándo? (when?), ¿cómo? (how?), ¿cuál! (which?), ¿cuánto? (how much?). It is demonstrative if it is used to answer a question: aquí (here), entonces (then), así (thus), tanto (so, so much), sí (yes). It is relative if it makes reference to an antecedent: donde (where), cuando (when), como (about), cuanto (as much as).

Examples:
interrogative

| ¿Dónde está mi chaqueta? | Where's my jacket? |

demonstrative

| Aquí nos vamos a quedar. | We are going to stay here. |

relative

| Aquí donde (relative) me ves. | Here where you see me. |

adverbio de adición – m / *adverb of addition*
Self-descriptive: además (also).

adverbio de afirmación – m / *adverb of affirmation* Self-descriptive: sí (yes), también (also), efectivamente (really), etc.

adverbio de cantidad – m / *adverb of quantity* Self-descriptive: bastante (enough), mucho (a lot), poco (little), muy (very), etc.

adverbio de duda – m / *adverb of doubt* Self-descriptive: quizá or quizás (maybe, perhaps), acaso (maybe, perhaps), etc.

adverbio de exclusión – m / *adverb of exclusion* Self-descriptive: tampoco (not…either).

adverbio de lugar – m / *adverb of place* Self-descriptive: aquí (here), allí (there), delante (in front), cerca (close), etc.

adverbio de modo – m / *adverb of manner* Self-descriptive: bien (well), mal (bad), mejor (better), despacio (slow), etc.

adverbio demostrativo – m / *demonstrative adverb* (See: adverbio correlativo)

adverbio de negación – m / *adverb of negation* Self-descriptive: jamás (never), no (no), tampoco (neither), etc.

adverbio de orden – m / *adverb of order* Self-descriptive: últimamente (lately), finalmente (finally), luego (later), etc.

adverbio de tiempo – m / *adverb of time* Self-descriptive: ayer (yesterday), antes (before), tarde (late), nunca (never), etc.

adverbio interrogativo – m / *interrogative adverb* (See: adverbio correlativo)

adverbio pronominal – m / *pronominal adverb* Denotes a substantive idea or a noun. For example: Vamos allá. (We are going there.) This phrase implies "a aquel lugar" (to that place).

adverbio relativo – m / (See: adverbio correlativo)

adyacente – adj / *adjacent* Adjective that qualifies or determines a noun.

aféresis – f / *apheresis* The elimination of a sound at the beginning of a word. For example, "norabuena" for "enhorabuena" (congratulations).

afijo – m / *affix* It is said of prefixes, infixes, and suffixes. Examples:

prefix: *hiper-* > hipersensible (hypersensitive)
infix: *-an-* > hume(an)te (smoking/steaming)
suffix: *-dad* > casualidad (chance)

afirmativo – adj / *affirmative* That affirms, like in the affirmative command:

¡Hazlo!	Do it!
¡Dámelo!	Give it to me!

Or in affirmative sentences, like:

La comida está lista.	The food is ready.
Juan va a la playa.	John is going to the beach.

Or in answers to questions, such as:

—¿Vas a trabajar hoy?	"Are you going to work today?"

—Sí, voy a trabajar hoy.	"Yes, I'm going to work today."

To make these sentences negative just place "no" before the verb, and in answering a question in the negative, use two negatives, as in:

—¿Vas a trabajar hoy?	"Are you going to work today?"
—No, no voy a trabajar hoy.	"No, I am not going to work today."
—¿Estudias alemán?	"Do you study German?"
—No, no estudio alemán.	"No, I don't study German."

áfono – adj / *aphonic/aphonous* A soundless, voiceless, unpronounced written letter. Example: In common speech, the *d* in "pared."

aforismo – m / *aphorism* Basically, a maxim; a short and pointed sentence expressing some significant truth or precept. An example (attributed to Leonardo da Vinci) is: Lo bueno no es siempre lo que es bello. (That which is beautiful is not always good.)

africada – adj / *affricate* (See: modo de articulación)

agente – adj / *agent* Designates the person, animal, or thing performing the action of the verb. Can also be used as a noun. Example: Mi casa fue inundada por las aguas. (My house was flooded by the waters.) In this case, "las aguas" is the agent.

aglutinación – **f** / *agglutination* The fusion of two or more words originally different into a single one. For example, in old Spanish: Cantar he. > Cantaré. (I will sing.); hac hora > ahora (now). Also, the accumulation of different affixes to express in some languages—like the Japanese—their grammatical relationship.

agramatical – **adj** / *non-grammatical* That doesn't follow the established grammatical norms.

aguda – **adj** / (See: acentuación)

alfabeto – **m** / (See: abecedario)

aliteración – **f** / *alliteration* In rhetoric, a figure consisting in repeating letters (usually consonants) at the beginning of two or more words adjacent to each other. Example: Federica, fría, fingida como siempre. (Federica, cold, false, as always.)

alófono – **adj** / *allophone* Any of the various forms of a phoneme as conditioned by adjoining sounds. In Spanish, as an adjective, it also means a person speaking a different language.

alveolar – **adj** / *alveolar* (See: punto de articulación)

ambigüedad – **f** / *ambiguity* The quality or state of being ambiguous, of having two or more possible meanings; hence, uncertain or vague.

Examples:

Salió y dejó la puerta como siempre.	He left and left the door as always.

A better sentence would have been: Salió y dejó la puerta abierta/cerrada, como siempre. (He left and left the door open/closed as always.)

Se puso el sombrero del lado que no era.	He put on his hat on the wrong side.

A better sentence would have been: Se puso el sombrero al revés. (He put on his hat backwards.)

americanismo – m / *Americanism* Word or expression belonging to or coming from an indigenous language of the Americas, like the Spanish "canoa" (canoe), "tomate" (tomato), "chocolate" (chocolate), "barbacoa" (barbecue).

anacoluto – m / *anacoluthon* Inconsistency or incoherence in the construction of speech, or changing in a sentence one grammatical construction for another. Examples:

anacoluto	**correct**
La mujer *que* su marido es abogado.	La mujer *cuyo* marido es abogado.

(The woman whose husband is a lawyer.)

Ellos creen *de que* no se les paga bien.	Ellos creen *que* no se les paga bien.

(They think that they are not getting paid enough.)

anadiplosis – f / *anadiplosis* In rhetoric, figure consisting in repeating the same word at the end of a sentence and at the beginning of the next. Example: Cansado, cansado estoy ya de tanto pensar. (Tired, tired I am of thinking so much.)

anáfora – f / *anaphora* In rhetoric, deliberate repetition of words or ideas. Example: Y llora la madre, llora, llora de alegría. (And the mother cries, cries, cries of happiness.)

anagrama – m / *anagram* Transposing or rearranging the letters in a word or phrase, which results in a different one. Example: dama > amad (lady > you love, informal plural).

analfabeto – adj / *illiterate* Incapable of reading or writing. Also, ignorant in any discipline.

analogía – f / *analogy* An explanation of something by comparing it or constrasting it with something else. Also, the creation of new linguistic forms (or modification of existing ones) similar to others. For example, the preterits "Tuve." (I had.); "Anduve." (I walked.); and "Estuve." (I was.) were formed by analogy of Hube. (I had. In the "pretérito anterior" tense.)

anáfora – f / *anaphora* A rhetorical figure in which the same word or words are repeated at the beginning of succeeding clauses. Example: ¿Dónde está mi inteligencia? ¿Dónde está mi ingenio? ¿Dónde está mi saber? (Where's my intelligence? Where's my ingenuity? Where's my knowledge?)

anástrofe – f / *anastrophe* In rhetoric, an inversion of the normal order of the parts of speech. For example, "De ganas lo hizo." (instead of "Lo hizo de ganas.") (He did it willingly.)

anécdota – f / *anecdote* Brief story used as an illustration or example or simply to entertain.

anfibología – f / *amphibology* A sentence conveying a second meaning due to a doubtful syntax. Example: Mando que mi heredero dé a mi acreedor diez monedas de oro, las que él quisiera. (I order that my heir give to my creditor ten gold coins, whichever ones he wants.) In this will, it is not clear what coins are chosen by the heir or by the creditor.

anglicismo – m / *Anglicism* The use of an English word or expression in another language, like in Spanish "closet" for "armario empotrado," "en términos de" (in terms of) for "en cuanto a," "láser" (laser), or the use of the gerund instead of the infinitive, as in "en llegando a" (upon arriving at) instead of "al llegar a," and in common idiomatic expressions such as "Que tenga un buen día." (Have a nice day.) instead of "Que le vaya bien." There are even English words that have been forced into the Spanish language by popular usage, such as "sofisticado" (sophisticated), which is the past participle of the verb "sofisticar" (originally meant "to adulterate" or "to falsify") or the use of "renta" (rent) for the better word "alquiler." Similarly, "complejo" is being used as in "a complex of factories or dwellings;" "facilidades" is used to mean "a company's facilities," such as buildings and other properties; and the overly-used "standard/estándard" or "doméstico" (domestic) is used in the sense of nation or national.

Anglicisms can also influence the spoken language; for example, misstressing Spanish words, such as "capital" on the syllable *CA* instead of *TAL*, or "metropolitano" on the syllable ME instead of TA. Numerous Spanish words in common usage in the United States are thus affected.

With the advent of technology, and especially computer science, hundreds of Anglicisms have found their way into Spanish, such as: internet, web, monitor, software, e-mail, mouse, and so on. Attempts have been made to come up with Spanish equivalents by digging deep into Greek and Latin roots, but the truth is that very few use them. One of the most awkward and meaningless Anglicisms in today's Spanish is the term "políticamente correcto" (politically correct), which requires defining it or explaining it due to its cultural context with no direct equivalent. "Políticamente correcto" means absolutely nothing in Spanish, aside from the fact that it combines an adverb and an adjective, which, although allowed grammatically—an adverb can qualify a verb, another adverb, or an adjective, as in "Pedro es excesivamente alto." (Peter is excessively tall.)—nonetheless lacks meaning and sounds very awkward. Politically correct terms abound in today's American English, such as "workforce" for "manpower," "police officer" for "policeman," "physically challenged" for "handicapped." In this regard, Spanish is lagging far behind.

angloamericanismo – m /*Anglo-Americanism*
Word or expression peculiar to the English spoken in the United States of America. Example: 24-7, meaning "24 hours a week."

anómalo – adj / *anomalous* Words that differ or deviate from the common grammatical rules in inflection. For example, the plural forms of Spanish words acquired from foreign languages, such as "bistecs" for "bistec" and "complots" for "complot."

antecedente – m / *antecedent* The noun referred to by the relative pronoun. Example: El niño que no estudia, tarde o temprano fracasará. (The child who doesn't study, sooner or later will fail.) Here, the antecedent of the relative pronoun "que" is the noun "el niño." The relative pronoun can be a subject, a direct or indirect object, a circumstantial complement, or a noun. Examples: Cada zapato huele al dueño que tiene. (Each shoe smells like its owner.—Direct object); La mujer a quien le dieron el regalo es muy agradecida. (The woman to whom they gave a present is very appreciative.—Indirect object); La casa donde vivo es de madera. (The house in which I live is made out of wood.—Circumstantial complement); El escritor publicó dos obras, una de las cuales se vendió mucho. (The author published two books, one of which sold very well.—Complement of the noun).

antítesis – f / *antithesis* In rhetoric, it consists in contraposing a word or phrase with another that has an opposite meaning. Example: Lloran los valientes y gozan los cobardes. (The brave moan and the cowards feast.)

antonomasia – f / *antonomasia* Figure consisting in using an epithet instead of the person's proper name. For example, "The Creator" for "God."

atenuación – f / *reduction/toning down* (See: litotes)

antónimo – m / *antonym* Word that expresses an opposite meaning, like: bueno > malo (good > bad), pena > alegría (sorrow > happiness), principio > fin (beginning > end).

apelativo – adj / *appellative* The same in Spanish as "sobrenombre," a name or nickname. Used also as a noun. Often added to the surname to distinguish two persons named the same. Example: José, hijo, José, padre (Joseph, junior, Joseph, senior).

apellido – m / *surname/last name* In Spanish, there are usually two last names for every person, the father's last name and the mother's maiden name, as in Federico Castroviejo Ramírez. Once married, some women keep their maiden name, as in Catalina Velasco Suárez, the "Suárez" being the maiden name. In the United States the woman's maiden name sometimes is hyphenated preceding the husband's last name, as in Emily Robertson-Williams. In this regard, there is no hyphenation in Spanish. The traditional courtesy titles in Spanish are "señor" (mister), "señora" (lady, madam), "señorita" (young woman). These are abbreviated "Sr." (Mr.), "Sra" (Mrs.), "Srta" (Miss). Traditionally, "señora" means a married woman, and "señorita" a single or unmarried woman. In abbreviation form, some use "Sa" for "Ms," although its usage is very limited in Spanish-speaking countries. Other titles of respect in

Spanish are "Don," "Doña," "doñito" for a young man, and "doñita" for a young woman (no direct English equivalents). All of these titles are used with the first name, as in Don/don Miguel, Doña/doña Caridad. When using the abbreviated forms "Sr." and "Sra.," the last name is always used, as in "Sr. López" (Mr. López), "Sra. Rodríguez" (Mrs. Rodríguez).

apócope – m / *apocope* The omission of the last letter or syllable of a word. Example: alguno > algún, voce > voz, Ana María > Mariana.

apodosis – f / *apodosis* (See: prótasis)

aposición – f / *apposition* Construction of two nominal elements, the second of which expresses something related to the first. Example: Lima, la capital del Perú, limita con el océano Pacífico. (Lima, the capital of Perú, borders with the Pacific Ocean.)

apóstrofo – m / *apostrophe* Orthographic symbol (') that indicates the elision of one letter or figure. It is not used in Spanish.

apotegma – m / *apothegm* A brief and pointed saying, usually from a famous person. For example, Descartes's "Pienso, luego existo." (I think, therefore I am.)

arabismo – m / *Arabism or Arabic word or expression* The use of an Arabic word or expression in another language, like in Spanish: "azúcar" (sugar), "¡ojalá!" (I wish), "alcalde" (mayor), "aceite" (oil).

arcaísmo – **m** / *archaism* Old word no longer in use; for example "desfacer" for "deshacer" (to undo).

argot – **m** / (See: jerga)

articulación – **f** / *articulation* The positioning of the organs of articulation for the distinct utterance of sounds by the human voice. The organs of articulation are divided into two groups: active and passive. The active organs include the lips, tongue, and soft palate or velum, and the passive comprise the upper teeth, alveolus, and hard palate.

artículo – **m** / *article* A word placed before the noun to enunciate its gender, number, and grammatical function. (See: artículo definido, artículo indefinido)

artículo definido – **m** / *definite article* Also called in Spanish "artículo determinado." Basically, Spanish has two definite articles, one masculine and the other feminine, with their corresponding plural forms:

masculine singular	**plural**
el	los

feminine singular	**plural**
la	las

The neuter form is "lo" (it).
All four correspond in English to "the." Articles, of course, always precede the noun, and are never used with other parts of speech (adjectives, verbs, etc.).

Examples:

Tengo el dinero en mi casa.	I have the money at home.
La niña es rubia.	The girl is blond.
Los hombres trabajan en el campo.	The men work in the field.
Las flores son muy bonitas.	The flowers are very beautiful.

There is a neuter article in Spanish, "lo," which is used mainly in substantive adjectives, such as "lo bello" (the beautiful), "lo bueno" (the good). It is important to know, however, that when the adjective refers to a particular person or thing (or several), the article agrees in gender and number with the name that person or thing would have, as in "el mayor," referring to the oldest brother, or "las viejas" (the old ones), referring to "las casas viejas" (the old houses).

artículo indefinido – m / *indefinite article* Also called "artículo indeterminado." Spanish has two indefinite articles, one masculine and the other feminine, with their corresponding plural forms:

masculine singular	**plural**
un	unos
feminine singular	**plural**
una	unas

In the singular, "un" and "una" correspond in English to "a" ("an" before words beginning with a vowel), and in the plural to "some." As with the definite articles, indefinite articles always precede the noun.

Examples:

Me dio un libro.	He/she gave me a book.
Se cayó una cuchara al suelo.	A spoon fell on the floor.
Se me acercaron unos hombres.	Some men approached me.
Unas niñas me lo contaron.	Some girls told me about it.

The indefinite article masculine singular ("un") cannot be confused with the adjective or number "uno" (one); therefore, it is incorrect to say "uno libro" (a book), "uno niño" (a boy/child).

asimilación – f / *assimilation* The process by which the articulation of a sound is modified, making it similar or identical to a neighboring one. For example, when the suffix *in* changes to *im* before *p*, as in "imposible" (impossible).

asíndeton – m / *asyndeton* A figure consisting in omitting a conjunction in coordinate sentences. Example: Vine, vi, vencí. (I came, I saw, I conquered.); Salgo, corro, vuelo a comprarte los zapatos. (I leave, run, fly to buy you the shoes.) (See also: oración coordinada)

atributo – m / *attribute/predicate* The role of the adjective within a nominal group; also, a term that qualifies or determines another using "ser," "estar," or another verb. Examples: Su amigo

Norberto era dentista. (His friend, Norberto, was a dentist.); La considero persona de confianza. (I consider her trustworthy.)

aún-aun – **adv** / *even-still* This word is written with an accent mark when it can be substituted by "todavía," as in: La casa aún está vacía. (The house is still empty.) "Aun" is devoid of written accent in all of the other cases, that is to say, when it is the equivalent of "también" (also), "hasta" (until), "inclusive" (including), and "ni siquiera" (not even). Both "aún" and "aun" are adverbs, and "aun" can also function at times as a preposition, as in: Aun sus padres lo sabían. (Even his/her parents knew it.)

B

barbarismo – m / *barbarism* The incorrect use of words or expressions in a language. For example, "Haiga" for "Haga" (That he/she may do); "Escribido" for "Escrito" (Written); "Jugan" for "Juegan" (They play).

bilabial – adj / *bilabial* (See: punto de articulación)

bilingüe – adj / *bilingual* Able to speak or write in two languages, provided each one is spoken and written well. In other words, being bilingual means having a good command of both languages in their spoken and written forms.

bisílabo – adj / *bi-syllable* A word having two syllables. Example: lo-bo (wolf), ma-dre (mother).

blasfemia – f / *blasphemy* Injurious word against God, the Virgin, or the Saints, or against someone who merits respect.

bosquejo – m / *outline* (See: esquema)

bucal – adj / *buccal* Belonging to or relative to the mouth.

C

cacofonía – f / *cacophony* In rethoric, a disagreeable sound of words caused by the unnecessary repetition of letters or syllables. Examples: La programación de ese canal de televisión no me gusta. (I don't like the programming of that television channel.); Que si aún queda queso no lo sé. (That if there is still cheese left, I don't know.)

cacología – f / *cacology* Expression that, without being grammatically incorrect, is considered substandard. In short, bad speaking and choice of words. For example, "Ese tipejo no hace más que jeringar." for "Ese hombre no hace más que molestar." (All that man does is to bother or be a pest.)

caló – m / *caló* The language spoken by the gypsies in Spain.

caso – m / *case* Inflection of the words contained in a sentence, each one expressing a different syntactical relationship. There are six cases:

ablativo (ablative)
Expresses the circumstantial complement of place, cause, manner, time, etc., and it is usually preceded by prepositions such as "con" (with), "de" (of), "desde" (since), "sin" (without), etc. Example: Me encontrarás en la oficina. (You'll find me in the office.)

acusativo (accusative)
Functions as the direct object. Example: El bombero apaga el incendio. (The fireman puts out the fire.)

dativo (dative)
Functions as the indirect object. Example: Pedro hace una pregunta al maestro. (Peter asks a question of the teacher.)

genitivo (genitive)
Functions as the complement of the noun, and it is usually preceded by the preposition "de" (of). Example: El carro de mi padre (the car of my father).

nominativo (nominative)
Corresponds to the subject of a sentence. Example: Margarita habla por teléfono. (Margarite talks on the phone.)

vocativo (vocative)
Serves to name or call a person or a personified object, and it is often preceded by the interjections "ah" or "oh." Example: ¡Oh, Laura, cuánto te extraño! (Oh, Laura, how much I miss you!)

castellano – m / *Castilian* Name also used for "Spanish," so named for having originated in the Kingdom of Castile, where it was spoken before Spain became a nation in the fifteenth century under the reign of the Catholic Kings. Some still claim, however, that the name "español" (Spanish) is inexact, as it leaves out many of the other languages spoken in Spain, such as catalán (Catalan), gallego (Galician), and vascuence (Basque).

In some Hispanic countries, such as Argentina, Chile, and Uruguay, the preferred name still is "castellano" for "Spanish."

casticismo – m / *quality of being "castizo" or pure, traditional* Of good origin and caste. A preference for using one's own traditional language, free of any foreign influence; also, typical, pure, genuine, of any country or region.

ceceo – m Pronouncing the *s* like the *c* before the *i, e,* or *z*. For example, "zemana" for "semana," "zabor" for "sabor."

circunlocución – f / *circumlocution* Roundabout or superlative speech, expressing with many words what could have been expressed with less or with just one. Example: Todo empezaba a quedarse en penumbras, sin esos rayos encendidos que tanto nos calentaban. (Everything began to get dark, without those bright rays that gave us so much warmth.) This phrase could easily be shortened to: Caía la tarde. (It was sunset.)

cláusula – f / *clause* Group of words that, having a complete meaning, contain one or more sentences intimately related to each other. Examples: Las casas en mi barrio son muy bonitas. (The houses in my neighborhood are very pretty.); Comemos en mi casa y a veces también en un restaurante. (We eat at home and sometimes also in a restaurant.) In Spanish, "clause" refers mainly to a subordinate sentence.

cognado – m / *cognate* Words that are written the same and have the same meaning in two languages. Examples in English and Spanish: piano, animal, hospital. There are also the "semi-cognados" (semi-cognates), which are words with similar spelling and equal meaning, such as: constitución (constitution), voto (vote), diccionario (dictionary). There are literally thousands of these words in English and Spanish, especially those derived from Greek and Latin.

coherencia – f / *coherence* Connection, relation, or union of parts or things to each other.

coma – f / *comma* Used to indicate a pause in writing.

comillas – m, pl / *quotation marks* Their meaning and use are the same in Spanish as in English. However, in Spanish, the period is placed after the closing quotation mark > ".

complemento – m / *complement* A word or group of words that complement the predicate or the subject. (See the various entries for different kinds of complements.)

complemento circunstancial – m / *circumstantial complement* In Spanish, it is the complement of the verb which can be of place, time, or manner. Example:

> **of place**
> Desde la ventana veo   From the window
> el jardín.   I see the garden.

"Desde la ventana" is the complement of place.

of time

En aquellos años trabajé duro.

In those years I worked hard.

"En aquellos años" is the complement of time.

of manner

Hice el trabajo de mala gana.

I did the work unwillingly.

"De mala gana" is the complement of manner.

The circumstantial complement can be:

a noun

Nos llamó desde Argentina.

He/she called us from Argentina.

a pronoun

Pensamos en ellos.

We think about them.

an infinitive with a preposition

Se cayó sin llorar.

He/she fell without crying.

a pronominal adverb

Subió las escaleras a tientas.

He/she felt his/her way up the stairs.

a whole sentence

Pospuso su cita porque tenía miedo.

He/she postponed his/her appointment out of fear.

complemento del predicado – m / *predicate complement* That which states something about a nominal element through a non-copulative verb. Examples: Llegó cansado. (He was tired when he arrived.); La nombraron presidenta. (She was named president.). They are: complemento directo (direct object), complemento indirecto (indirect object), complemento circunstancial (circumstantial complement), each one with their respective complements. (See each entry.)

complemento del sujeto – m / *subject complement* The subject can be a single noun or a series of words expressing a concept to complete its meaning. Example: Los edificios de Nueva York son muy altos. (The buildings in New York are very tall.) Here, "los edificios de Nueva York" is the subject, referring not to any buildings but specifically to those in New York.

complemento directo – m/ *direct object* The person or thing receiving the direct action of the verb, or that which expresses what the verb does. Examples: Veo el carro. (I see the car.); Compramos los zapatos. (We buy the shoes.); Terminaré el trabajo mañana. (I will finish the work tomorrow.) In the first sentence, the direct object is "el carro," in the second it is "los zapatos," and in the third it is "el trabajo." (See also: pronombre de complemento directo) An easy way to find out the direct object in a sentence is by asking the verb within the sentence, that is, by using "¿Qué?" (What?) for things, and "¿Quién?" (Who?) for persons. Examples: Lavo el carro. (I wash the car.) Question: What do I wash? > the car. Veo a María. (I see Mary.) Question: Who do I see? > Mary. The direct object can be preceded by the preposition "a" or by no preposition, and could be used before animals or personified objects, as in: Veo al gato. (I see the cat.); Honro a la humildad. (I honor humility.) (See also: a personal) In transitive sentences, the direct object can be:

a noun with preposition

La gente trabaja en la oficina.

People work in the office.

a noun using the preposition "a"

Ella quiere mucho a sus hijos.

She loves her children very much.

an unstressed pronoun

Me caí por las escaleras.

I fell down the stairs.

a pronoun preceded by the preposition "a"

No llamaré a nadie.

I won't call anybody.

a verb in the infinitive

Ellos quieren salir.

They want to leave.

a whole sentence

Necesitan que vengas en seguida.

They need for you to come right away.

a pronominal adverb

Yo no tenía suficiente.

I didn't have enough. (Referring to "dinero," money.)

complemento indirecto – m / *indirect object*

The word or group of words denoting the person or thing indirectly receiving the action of the verb. Examples: Dale a Juan la pelota. (Give John the ball); Este regalo es para mi madre. (This present is for my mother.) In Spanish, it is always preceded by the prepositions "a" (to) or "para" (for). In fact, there cannot be an indirect object without using either one of these prepositions. An easy way to find out the indirect object in a sentence is by asking the verb "¿a quién?" or "¿para quién?" (to whom or for whom?). In the above examples "Juan" and "mi madre" are the indirect objects. Indirect object pronouns usually precede the conjugated verb, as in: Le doy la pelota a Juan. (I give the ball to John.) (See also: pronombre de complemento directo and pronombre de complemento indirecto) The indirect object can be:

a noun

Le hizo una pregunta a su amigo.

He/she asked a question of his/her friend.

an unstressed pronoun

Nos dieron la bienvenida.

They welcomed us.

a pronoun preceded by a preposition

No dejó ningún paquete para ellos.

He/she didn't leave any package for them.

an infinitive verb

Me fui al campo para descansar mejor.

I went to the country to rest better.

a whole sentence

Estudia para que te respeten.

Study so they can respect you.

composición – f / *composition* The formation of words by joining two words with or without morphological variance, such as "espantapájaros" (scarecrow), "matamoscas" (flyswatter).

concordancia – f / *agreement/concord* Agreement between variable words in the construction of sentences, such as adjectives with nouns in gender and number, and verbs with nouns or pronouns in number and person. In Spanish, this agreement is necessary, especially when using nouns and adjectives. Examples: La manzana es roja. (The apple is red.); Toda la ciudad está iluminada. (The entire city is illuminated.); Ellos están ocupados. (They are busy.)

conjugación – **f** / *conjugation* A methodical exposition or arrangement of the inflectional forms of a verb, indicating its mood, tense, number, and person. Example: conjugation in the present indicative:

hablar	**to speak**
hablo	I speak
hablas	you speak
habla	he/she speaks/you speak (formal singular)
hablamos	we speak
habláis	you speak
hablan	they speak/you speak (formal plural)

hablo, hablas, habla are singular forms
hablamos, habláis, hablan are plural forms
hablo is the first person singular
hablas is the second person singular
habla is the third person singular
hablamos is the first person plural
habláis is the second person plural
hablan is the third person plural
other inflectional forms
hablé > indicative, preterit, singular, first person
hablaba > indicative, imperfect, singular, first person/third person

hablaré > indicative, future, singular, first person

hablaría > conditional simple, singular, first person

he hablado > indicative, present perfect, singular, first person

había hablado > indicative, past perfect/pluperfect singular, first person

hube hablado > indicative, past perfect, singular, first person

habré hablado > indicative, future perfect, singular, first person

habría hablado > indicative, conditional perfect, singular, first person

hable > subjunctive, present, singular, first person

hablara > subjunctive, imperfect, singular, first person

hubiera/hubiese hablado > subjunctive, past perfect/pluperfect, singular, first person

¡hable! > command (speak!), singular, second person, formal.

(See also: conjugación verbal)

Let's analyze these two sentences in terms of their mood and tenses:

Hoy no me baño porque me bañé ayer, pero me bañaré mañana. (I don't bathe today because I bathed yesterday, but I will bathe tomorrow.) Here, all three verbs, "baño," "bañé," and "bañaré," belong to the indicative mood, and are, respectively, the present tense, the preterit tense, and the future tense. Now let's see this other sentence:

Es probable que hoy me bañe, pero si no me bañara, me bañaría mañana. (It is probable that I will bathe today, but if I don't bathe, I would bathe tomorrow.) Here, the first verb, "bañe" is the first person singular of the subjunctive mood, "bañara" is the imperfect tense also of the subjunctive mood, and "bañaría" is the first person singular of the conditional simple.

conjugación perifrástica – f / *periphrastic conjugation* The one formed by an auxiliary verb instead of by inflection. Example using the verb "estudiar" (to study): Tengo que estudiar. (I have to study.)

conjunción – f / *conjunction* A word used to connect sentences, phrases, clauses, or words. They can be simple, "y" (and), "pues" (then), or compound, "con tal que" (provided that), "puesto que" (since). Some conjunctions can also function as adverbs, like "ahora que" (now that), "mientras" (while), "ya" (already).

conjunción adversativa – f / *adversative conjunction* Denotes opposition between the preceding sentence and the one following it. For example, "pero" (but).

conjunción causal – f / *causal conjunction* That preceding the sentence that brings about what has been expressed in the main sentence. For example, "porque" (because).

conjunción comparativa – f / *comparative conjunction* Denotes comparison. For example, "como" (like).

conjunción condicional – f / *conditional conjunction* Denotes condition or the necessity of verification of some circumstance. For example, "si" (if), "siempre que" (whenever), "así como" (while).

conjunción consecutiva-continuativa – f / *consecutive conjunction* The one implying or denoting continuation. Example: Ya te he dicho, pues, que la farmacia está cerrada. (Well, I have already told you that the pharmacy is closed.)

conjunción coordinante – f / *coordinating conjunction* The one linking two elements of a sentence performing the same function, like: Samuel es médico y enfermero. (Samuel is a doctor and a nurse.) To the same group belong the copulative, disjunctive, adversative, causal, ilative, and consecutive conjunctions.

conjunción copulativa – f / *copulative conjunction* Coordinates sequentially a sentence with another. For example, "y" (and), "ni" (nor/or).

conjunción disyuntiva – f / *disjunctive conjunction* Indicates a contrast, an alternative, or a contraposition between two or more persons, things, or ideas. For example, "o" (or).

conjunción ilativa – f / *illative conjunction* Used in subordinate sentences in which the second sentence signals the consequence that is deduced from the first. Some of these conjunctions or equivalent adverbial conjunctions are: luego (then), conque (so), así (thus), por lo tanto (therefore). Examples: Yo no iría; por lo tanto, tú tampoco deberías ir. (I wounld't go; therefore, you shouldn't go either.); No tengo tiempo; por lo tanto, para de insistir. (I have no time; therefore, stop asking.)

conjunción simple/coordinante – f / *simple/ coordinating conjunction* Consisting of one word. Examples: y (and), pero (but), o (or), sino (but), luego (therefore), pues (well/then/as/since).

conjunción compuesta – f / *compound conjunction* Consisting of a group of words equivalent to a conjunction. For example, "con tal que" (provided that), "para que" (in order to).

conjunción subordinante – f / *subordinating conjunction* The one introducing a preposition in a sentence, such as "que" (that), "si" (if), "pues" (well/the/as/since). Subordinating conjunctions can also be formed in a group using "que" (that) with various prepositions, like "para que" (so that), "a fin de que" (in order to), "aparte de que" (apart from), "hasta que" (until/till), or fused together, such as "aunque" (although), "porque" (because).

connotación – f / *connotation* What a word suggests or implies. For example, the word "mosquito" may imply or suggest "infection," "malaria," "death."

conque-con que – conj / *so* It is written as one word when it is a simple conjunction, and as two words when it is a circumstantial complement and can be substituted by "el," "la," or "cual." Example of the first: Ya sé que andas despacio, conque apúrate. (I know you are slow, so hurry up.) Example of the second: Según el espacio con que se cuente. (According to the space that one may have.) At times, "con que" can be substituted by the conditional "si" (if), and a word may be inserted between the "con" and the "que," as in: Con solo que lo hagas. (Provided that you do it.)

consonante – f / *consonant* Any of the 24 letters of the Spanish alphabet minus the vowels.

contexto – m / *context* The parts of a sentence or paragraph that occur just prior to or following a specified word or passage and determine its precise meaning. In other words, the meaning of certain words depends on how they are used and in what context. For example, the adjective "negro" (black), which can refer just to the color or to a whole race, as in: Mi abrigo es negro. (My coat is black.); La población negra de Estados Unidos sobrepasa el 20% del total. (The Black population in the United States exceeds 20% of the total.)

contracción – f / *contraction* The fusion of two words into a single one, the second of which usually begins with a vowel, like "al" < "a el," "del" < "de el." However, this contraction only occurs in the case of the definitite article "el" and not of the pronoun "él," meaning "him," in which case there is no contraction: Lo veo a él. (I see him.); Ese libro es de él. (That book is his.)

cópula – f / *copula* A term linking the subject with the predicate, especially the conjunctions and copulative verbs, such as "ser" (to be) or "estar" (to be). Example: Mi padre está apurado. (My father is in a hurry.)

corchete – m / *bracket* ([ ]) Either of these two signs used to enclose explanatory matter.

correlación gramatical – f / *grammatical correlation* The one established between two phrasal terms, in such a way that the use of one requires the use of the other, whether being elliptic or expressed. Example: Como padre, como hijo, no sólo es cabezón sino majadero. (Like father, like son, not only is he hard-headed but whiny as well.)

cuerdas vocales – f, pl / *vocal cords* Either of two pairs of bands or folds located in the larynx. Only the lower pair vibrates, producing vocal sounds passed up from the lungs.

cultismo – m / *learned word/expression* Word, usually of Greek or Latin origin, used in intellectual, literary, or scientific language. For example, "Dios" (God, from "Deus"), "espíritu" (spirit, from "spiritum"), "siglo" (century, from "saeculum").

D

declinación – f / *declension* The inflection of words, such as nouns, pronouns, and adjectives, manifested in the change of endings to express their different relations of gender, person, number, and case. The declension is typical of all Spanish verbs, pronouns, and most adjectives. Examples: Yo estudio inglés y ella estudia alemán. (I study English and she studies German.); La tienda es mía. (The store is mine.); La ventana está abierta. (The window is open.) The declension of the adjective can be done only when it is used together with the noun and in a substantival form, and also as a substantival neuter. Example:

nominative:	el rico (the rich)
genitive:	del rico (of the rich)
dative:	al o para el rico (to or for the rich)
acussative:	el rico o al rico (the rich or to the rich)
vocative:	el rico (the rich), or ¡oh el rico! (oh, the rich!)
ablative:	con, de, en (etc.) el rico (with, of, or in the rich)

deixis – f / *deixis* A word whose meaning within a phrase requires specific contextual information. For example, the sentence "Me rompí el dedo." (I broke my finger.) requires a description of which finger it is.

denotación – f / *denotation* Refers to the actual or precise meaning of a word as described in a dictionary.

dental – adj / *dental* (See: punto de articulación)

derivado – m / *derivative* Said of a word that has been formed by derivation, such as "electricidad" (electricity) from "eléctrico" (electric), "campanario" (bell tower) from "campana" (bell), "caballero" (knight) from "caballo" (horse), "ciudadano" (citizen) from "ciudad" (city).

desinencia – f / *ending* Affix that is added to the root of a word indicating various grammatical aspects such as gender, number, person, case, tense, and mood; for example, the ending *-ando* to form the gerund of *AR* verbs, or the *a* to form the feminine of the word "abuelo" > "abuela."

dialecto – m / *dialect* In broad terms, a dialect is a regional/geographical variation of a language that mainly affects its pronunciation but rarely its vocabulary or morphology. In Spain, some of the dialects are extremeño, andaluz, canario, and murciano, whereas gallego and catalán, once considered dialects also, have now been officially declared languages.

diálogo – m / *dialogue* Conversation between two or more persons.

dicción – f / *diction* Manner of speaking that can be good or bad depending on the correct or incorrect use of words and constructions.

dicho – m / *saying* A phrase containing a popular maxim, such as: Saber es poder. (Knowledge is power.) As in any other language, there are thousands upon thousands of "dichos" in Spanish, depending on the country or region.

diccionario – m / *dictionary* Book listing and explaining in orderly fashion words of one or more languages, a science, or a particular subject matter.

diéresis – m / *diaeresis* Orthographical symbol placed over the *ü* in the combinations *gue, gui,* so that letter can be pronounced, as in "cigüeña," "vergüenza."

diglosia – f / *diglossia* Bilinguism, especially when one of the languages is considered socially and politically superior.

diptongo – m / *diphthong* In Spanish, any combination of a strong vowel (*a,e,o*) and a weak vowel (*i,u,* and also *y*). The Spanish language has a total of 14 diphthongs:

diphthong	word
ai (ay)	bailar, hay
ei (ey)	aceituna, ley
oi (oy)	heroico, hoy
ui (uy)	ruina, ¡huy!
au	audio
eu	deuda
ou*	Bouza
ia	limpia
ie	miedo
io	ripio

iu	ciudadano
ua	lenguaje
ue	juego
uo	continuo

*Ou diphthongs are mostly used in words derived from Portuguese or Galician.

In diphthongs, the stress always falls on the strong vowel unless there is a written accent mark over the weak vowel, as in: dí-a, dú-o, which splits it into two syllables. If there is a written accent mark over the strong vowel, as in: sabéis, cantáis, the syllable is not split.

disimilación – **f** / *dissimilation* Altering the articulation of a speech sound, which causes it to be different from a continuous or neighboring one. For example, "rarus" (Latin) > "raro" (Spanish), "carcere" (Latin) > "cárcel" (Spanish).

disonancia – **f** / *dissonance* Harsh, disagreeable sound.

dos puntos – **m, pl** / *colon (:)* It denotes a long pause. It is different from the period in that it is always followed by a clarification or continuation.

E

elipsis – f / *ellipsis* The omission of a word or words in a sentence that may be deemed unnecessary to render its complete meaning. Example: Hemos comprado una casa parecida a la que mi hermana ha comprado. (We have bought a house similar to the one that my sister has bought.) The "ha comprado" in Spanish and "has bought" in English are unnecessary to complete the construction and thus be understood. Elliptical construction would render this sentence as: Compramos una casa parecida a la de mi hermana. (We have bought a house similar to my sister's.)

elisión – f / *elision* The suppression of a vowel at the end of a word when the one that follows begins with another vowel. For example, "del" for "de el" (of the). Also, the supression of some linguistic element in speech without contradicting the grammatical rules. Example: Mi cuñado trabaja en Lima y mi cuñada (trabaja) en Quito. (My brother-in-law works in Lima and my sister-in-law (works) in Quito.)

elocución – f / *elocution/speech* A manner of speaking to express concepts, especially in public; also, language, expression, style.

enálage – f / *enallage* The use of one part of speech or inflection for another. For example, "Comienzo a trabajar en una semana." (I start working in one week.) instead of saying "Empezaré a trabajar en una semana." (I will start working in one week.)

enclisis – f / *enclisis* The union of one or more unstressed words with another stressed word. Example: Dáselo. (Give it to him/her.) There is enclisis in *se* and *lo*.

enclítica, palabra – f / *enclitic, word* (See: proclítica, palabra)

enlace – m / *union/link* The usual linking words in Spanish are the prepositions, conjunctions, and relative pronouns. Examples: Voy a la fiesta con mi amigo. (I go to the party with my friend.); Me gustaría ir pero no puedo. (I would like to go but I can't.); Espero que me llames esta noche. (I hope that you call me tonight.) The linking words here are "con" (with), "pero" (but), and "que" (that).

en seguida-enseguida – adv / *at once/right away* It can be written either way, as one or two words.

entonación – f / *intonation* Pitch or tone in the succession of sounds corresponding to a word, phrase, or any fragment of speech.

enunciado – m / *statement* The sequence of words marked by pauses that can be constituted by one or more sentences. Example: Los ríos de mi pueblo, chicos, serenos, cristalinos, en los que de niño me bañaba. (The rivers of my town, small, serene, crystalline, in which I used to bathe when I was a child.)

epanadiplosis – f / *epanadiplosis* Figure of rhetoric consisting in repeating at the end of a sentence or phrase the same word used at the beginning. Example: La flor se marchita, la última flor. (The flower withers, the last flower.)

epéntesis – f / *epenthesis* Figure of speech consisting in adding a letter or syllable to the middle of a word. For example, "pónete" for "ponte" (put on), "corónica" for "crónica" (chronicle).

epiceno, nombre – m / *epicene* A common noun that has the same gender to designate both sexes, like: víctima (victim), bebé (baby), ardilla (squirrel), buitre (vulture).

epíteto – m / *epithet* An adjective expressing a certain characteristic quality of that to which it is applied. Example: El sabio maestro (the wise teacher). If "sabio" would be used as a modifying adjective, it would follow the noun, as in: El maestro sabio.

esbozo – m / *outline* (See: esquema)

escritura – f / *writing* The art of writing, which can be a letter, document, or any kind of written paper.

esdrújula – adj / (See: acentuación)

español antiguo – m / *old Spanish* Spoken on the Iberian Peninsula from approximately the tenth to the beginning of the fifteenth centuries. In morphology and syntax, one of its characteristics was the use of the verb "ser" as an auxiliary verb to form perfect tenses instead of the modern form of "haber." For example, "Las mugeres son llegadas." instead of "Las mujeres han llegado." (Note that the past participle agrees in gender and number with the subject.) Other words were "omne" for "hombre" (man), "muger" for "mujer" (woman), "do" for "donde" (where), as in: "Por do caminamos." instead of "Por donde caminamos." Phonetically, the sound of [x] of modern Spanish (voiceless velar fricative) of the *j* and the *g* before *e, i* did not exist in Old Spanish, nor did the sound of the *th* as pronounced in the region of Castile, as in "cabeza," "acero." One of the best examples of Old Spanish is the *Poema del Cid,* written about 1140. Miguel de Cervantes, the author of *Don Quijote,* was instrumental in the transition from Old Spanish to modern Spanish, just like Shakespeare was to English.

esquema – m / *outline* Summary of writings or speeches setting down only their most significant characteristics.

etcétera – f / *etcetera* From the Latin meaning "y lo demás" (and so on and so forth), abbreviated in both English and Spanish "etc."

etimología – f / *etymology* The origin of words, why they came about, their meanings and forms. For example, "azucena" from the Hispanic-Arabic "asussána" (white lily), "guerra" from the Germanic "werra" (fight, discord), "barbacoa" (barbecue), perhaps from the Taino language (sticks placed over a hole to roast meat), "madre" from the Latin "mater-tris" (mother), "clóset" from the English "closet" (small enclosure) and this from the Latin "clausum" (closed space).

eufemismo – m / *euphemism* A word or phrase meant to soften a direct and frank expression that may result in being harsh and offensive. For example, "tercera edad" instead of "anciano" (old person), "físicamente afectado" instead of "inválido" (handicapped), "daños colaterales" instead of "víctimas civiles" (civil casualties), "étnico" instead of "negro" or "indio" (Black, Indian).

eufonía – f / *euphony* Combination of agreeable sounds in speech or music. The opposite of "cacophony." Example: bello amanecer, tranquilo, sereno, animoso (beautiful dawn, tranquil, serene, spirited).

exégesis – f / *exegesis* An explanation or interpretation.

expletivo – adj / *expletive* A word or phrase not really necessary, but one that is added for rhetorical purposes to embellish an expression. Examples: No me voy hasta que no me echen a patadas. (I won't leave until they kick me out.); Mi familia ha tenido mil contratiempos. (My family has gone through a thousand setbacks.) (See also: jerga)

explosiva – adj / *explosive* Said of a consonant, usually occlusive, pronounced with a sudden release of breath. In Spanish, it is said that the *p* in "pato" (duck), or the *s* in "sumar" (to add) are explosive. Nothing compared, however, to the explosion of such English consonants as the *p* or *t* as in "Pete" or "Tom."

expresión – f / *expression* Thoughts or ideas. Also, a word, phrase, or sentence used in an idiomatic expression, such as "agarrar una pulmonía" (to catch pneumonia).

extranjerismo – m / *foreign origin* Word, phrase, or expression that a language takes from another. For example, "turista" (tourist) was taken from English, "embajada" (embassy) was taken from Italian, and "jardín" (garden) was taken from French.

F

factitivo – adj / *factitive* (See: verbo causativo)

falta de ortografía – f / *spelling error* Spelling mistake. Also called "orthographical error."

familia de lenguas – f / *family of languages* Group of languages deriving from one language, like "the family of Romance Languages" (Spanish, French, Italian, Portuguese, etc.) derive from Latin.

familia de palabras – f / *family of words* All the words etymologically derived from the same root, like "capital" (capital), "capitalino" (from the capital), "capitalista" (capitalist), "capitalismo" (capitalism).

femenino – adj / *feminine* Refers to one of the two genders in Spanish, usually nouns ending in *a*, like "la pluma" (the pen), "la playa" (the beach). In words ending in any of the other vowels or in a consonant, the gender is determined by the definite article, like "la noche" (the night), "la sal" (the salt), "la ciudad" (the city). There are also some words beginning with *a* that take the masculine article "el" to avoid clashing in pronunciation, such as "el agua" (the water, instead of "la agua"), but that are feminine when modified by adjectives, such as: El agua es pura. (The water is pure.), and likewise with "alma" (soul), taking the masculine article "el" ("el alma" instead of "la alma"), as in: El alma es eterna. (The soul is eternal.) instead of La alma es eterna. This lends itself to widespread confusion; for example, in the case of the demonstrative adjectives, in which both the masculine and the feminine are used indistinctively, as in "ese agua," "esa agua" (that water), but take always the feminine form when modified by adjectives, as in: Esa agua es pura. (That water is pure.)

figura de construcción – f / *figure of construction* They are five in total: hyperbaton (hyperbaton), elipsis (ellipsis), pleonasmo (pleonasm), silepsis (syllepsis), and traslación (enallage). (See each one separately.)

filología – f / *philology* The science studying a culture as manifested in its language and literature, especially through written records.

flexión – f / *inflection* The change that occurs in words by using different endings, or the vowel change that occurs in the stem of some verbs. For example, in Spanish, the *o* of the verb "poder" that changes to *ue* when conjugated in the first person singular of the present indicative ("puedo"), or the ending *emos* in the first person plural of "hablar" in the present subjunctive (*amos* in the present indicative).

fonación – f / *phonation* Sound, the voice, the emission of a word.

fonema – m / *phoneme* Each of the simple sounds into which the spoken language can be broken down, and also the graphic symbol used to represent it writing. In Spanish, there are 24 phonemes; among them: /a/, /f/, /s/, /ñ/.

fonética – f / *phonetics* The study of the real sounds or speech of a language.

fonología – f / *phonology* The systematic study of the evolution of speech sounds of a language.

formal – adj / *formal* Refers mainly to the formal form of address in Spanish, indicated by the endings of the third person singular or the third person plural of all verbs in all moods and tenses. For example, use of the formal "you" in the present indicative of "cantar" ("canta" and "cantan") requires using "usted" or "ustedes." Note, however, that in most Spanish-speaking countries today the third person plural is indistinctively used for both the informal and formal plurals. Example: ¿Dónde van a comer hoy? (Where are you going to eat today?) instead of differentiating between ¿Dónde vais a comer hoy? (informal plural) and ¿Dónde van a comer hoy? (formal plural). Outside of Spain, this second person plural ("vosotros") is seldom used in Hispanic countries, although most people understand what it means. Should we then use it? It all depends. From a traditional point of view, yes; from a practical point of view, no, or perhaps. Is it used in the Spanish spoken in the United States today? No.

frase – f / *phrase* Group of words that would suffice to have a meaning without constituting a sentence; in other words, lacking a subject and a predicate. Example: Como anillo al dedo (like a ring to the finger).

frase adverbial – **f /** *adverbial phrase* (See: locución adverbial)

frase de cortesía – **f /** *courtesy phrase* Meant to express deference and respect when addressing somebody. Example: con permiso (excuse me), bienvenido (welcome), gracias (thank you), saludos (greetings).

fricativa – **adj /** *fricative* (See: modo de articulación)

función – **f /** *function* Related role that, in the grammatical structure of a sentence, is performed by a phonic, morphological, lexical, or syntagmatic element.

futuro imperfecto – **m /** *future* It is formed by adding to the whole infinitive a set of endings that are the same for all three main conjugations (*AR, ER, IR*). For example, the verb "escribir" (to write), which belongs to the third conjugation (*IR*-ending):

Spanish	**English**
escribiré	I will write
escribirás	you will write
escribirá	he/she will write
escribiremos	we will write
escribiréis	you will write
escribirán	they will write

The same endings (*é, ás, á, emos, éis, án*) apply to all verbs ending in *AR* or *ER* as well. Example:

Cantaré. (I will sing.) from "cantar," Comeré. (I will eat.) from "comer," etc. (See also: modo indicativo)

futuro perfecto – m / *future perfect* Expresses a future action taking place before another future action, as in: Cuando me llamen ya habré comido. (I will have eaten by the time they call me.) Here, the action of eating is prior to their calling. It is formed by the future tense of the auxiliary verb "haber" (to have, which is irregular) plus a past participle. Example of the verb "llamar" (to call) conjugated in the future perfect:

Spanish	English
habré llamado	I will have called
habrás llamado	you will have called
habrá llamado	he/she will have called
habremos llamado	we will have called
habréis llamado	you will have called
habrán llamado	they will have called

(See also: modo indicativo)

G

galicismo – m / *Gallicism* The use of a French word in another language. Examples: chef, chalet, boutique, biscuit (French words also used in English). "Debutar" (to make one's debut) is also a Gallicism, now fully integrated into the Spanish language.

género – m / *gender* In Spanish, the masculinity or femininity of nouns, such as: el abrigo (the coat), la mesa (the table). Many nouns, however, don't end in *o* or *a* for the masculine or feminine, respectively, in which case the definite article determines the gender. Examples: el árbol (the tree, masculine), la flor (the flower, feminine).

gerundio – m / *gerund* The one form with the ending *ando*, for verbs ending in *AR*, and *iendo*, for verbs ending in *ER/IR*, as in: "caminando" (walking), "comiendo" (eating), "escribiendo" (writing). It is also called "gerundio simple" (simple gerund), and is always invariable. Usually, the gerund in Spanish is used with the verb "estar," as in: Están trabajando. (They are working.); Estoy durmiendo. (I am sleeping.)

gerundio compuesto – m / *compound gerund* The one used with the helping verb "haber" (to have), as in "habiendo trabajado" (having worked).

giro – **m** / *expression* Special structure of the phrase, or the manner in which words are organized in order to express a concept.

glosario – **m** / *glossary* A vocabulary listing the words of a science or art book, author, etc. duly defined and commented. Example: Glosario médico (Medical Glossary).

grado – **m** / *degree* Manner to signify the relative intensity of the qualifiers.

grafía – **f** / *spelling* The act of forming words, of putting them together, or orthography.

gramática – **f** / *grammar* The rules and precepts that govern the correct use of a language.

gramática comparada – **f** / *comparative grammar* That which studies the relationship that could be established between one or more languages.

gramática descriptiva – **f** / *descriptive grammar* That dealing with the synchronic study of a language.

gramática estructural – **f** / *structural grammar* The study of a language based on the principle that all of its elements are systematically interrelated.

gramática funcional – **f** / *functional grammar* The study of the functions of each of the elements that make up a language.

gramática histórica – **f** / *historical grammar* That which studies the evolution of a language through time.

gramática normativa – f / *normative grammar*
That which defines the correct uses of a language through precepts.

grave / llana – adj / (See: acentuación)

grupo verbal – m / *verb group* That which is constructed around a verb. Example: Lanzar el balón. (To throw the ball.)

guión – m / *dash/hyphen (-)* Used to join the two parts of some compound words. Example: Comercio arábigo-hispánico (Arabic-Hispanic commerce).

gutural – adj / *guttural* A sound produced by placing the back of the tongue near or against the soft palate or velum. (See: uvular)

H

había-habían – v / When the verb "haber" is used in an impersonal form and is applied to the existence of something, it is always used in the singular even though its complement may be in the plural. Example: En la fiesta había muchos invitados. (In the party there were many guests.) instead of En la fiesta habían muchos invitados. According to Andrés Bello, such a mistake is quite common in speech and should be avoided.

habla – m / *speech* The art of speaking, of communicating thoughts and feelings through the spoken word and vocal sounds.

hablante – m / *speaker* A person who speaks.

haplología – f / *haplology* The elimination of a syllable similar to a continous one within the same word. Example: Latin > idololatres, Spanish > idólatra.

hay – / *there is/there are* Second form of the third person singular of the present indicative of the verb "haber" (to have). It is used as a transitive verb. Example: En esta clase hay muchos estudiantes. (In this classroom there are many students.)

he – adv / *here* Besides being the first person singular of the verb "haber" (to have) used in the present perfect of the indicative, "he" is also an adverb that, combined with the pronouns "me," "te," "la," "le," "lo," "las," "los," serves to indicate a person or thing. Examples: Heme aquí. (Here I am.); Helos aquí. (Here they are.) However, this construction is rare and is mostly used in Spain.

heteronimia – f / *heteronym* Words with identical spellings but totally different meanings. For example, "la herida" (wound, noun) and "herida" (wounded, adjective), as in: Me duele la herida. (The wound hurts.); La mujer está herida. (The woman is wounded.) Another example is "el enfermo" (sick/ill person, noun) and "enfermo" (sick/ill, adjective).

hiato – m / *hiatus* Basically, a pause in pronunciation. It consists of separating two adjacent vowels, thus forming two separate syllables instead of one. It is the opposite of the "sinéresis" (see). Example: su-a-ve for sua-ve (three syllables instead of two). It also affects the synalepha. (See: sinalefa)

hipérbaton – m / *hyperbaton* A change or transposition in the logical order of words in a sentence. Example: Josefina le da a su madre por su cumpleaños el regalo. (Instead of "Josefina le da el regalo a su madre por su cumpleaños.") (Josephine gives the present to her mother for her birthday.) The logical syntactical order in Spanish is subject + verb + direct object + indirect object + circumstantial complement; however, in that sentence, the order is transposed as follows: subject + verb + indirect object + circumstantial complement + direct object. Either sentence would be understood, but, syntactically speaking, the first one doesn't follow the established norm, making it harder to understand. The same ambiguity would happen in English if one would say: Josephine gives to her mother the present for her birthday. Such a sentence would alter the logical syntactical order. However, in using direct and indirect object pronouns, the syntactical order is essential to convey meaning. In Spanish it would be: Se lo da por su cumpleaños. and in English: He gives it to her for her birthday. Here, the formula in Spanish is: indirect object pronoun + direct object pronoun + verb, and in English, just the reverse: verb + direct object pronoun + indirect object pronoun. Altering the order here would render that sentence meaningless in either language.

hipérbole – f / *hyperbole* Figure consisting of exaggerating something to create an effect. It is not meant to be taken seriously. Example: Este hombre es tan viejo como Matusalén. (This man is as old as Methuselah.)

hipónimo – m / *hyponym* Word whose meaning is included in another one. For example, "mosquito" respecting "insect," "golondrina" (swallow) respecting "bird."

hipotaxis – f / *hypotaxis* Subordination in a grammatical construction. Example: El niño juega y su hermana lo mira. (The boy plays and his sister watches him.); La puerta por la que entraste está rota. (The door through which you came in is broken.)

hispanohablante – **adj** / *Spanish-speaking* A native speaker of Spanish, or a person for whom Spanish is his/her mother tongue.

homófono – **adj** / *homophone* Refers to a word sounding like another but with a different meaning. For example, "tuvo" (verb, he/she had), and "tubo" (noun, tube).

homógrafo – **adj** / *homograph* Refers to a word written like another but with a different meaning. Example: sobre (about), sobre (envelope).

homónimo – **m** / *homonym* Said of words written the same but having a different meaning. Examples:

cura (priest)	cura (cure)
corte (cut)	corte (court)
cuna (crib)	cuna (birthplace/ cradle)
coma (coma)	coma (comma)

idiotismo – m / *idiotism* Phrase or expression that doesn't follow the established grammatical rules. Example: a lengua chismes (with the tongue, gossip).

improperio – m / *expletive word* The same as "palabrota" in Spanish. (See also: jerga)

inciso – m / *interpolated clause* Expression that is inserted inside another independently, to explain something with which it is related. Also called in Spanish "oración incidental" (incidental sentence). Example: Ella—según me ha dicho—vendrá con nosotros. (She—according to what she has told me—will come with us.) (See also: paréntesis)

incoherencia – f / *incoherence* The opposite of "coherencia" (coherence). (See)

incongruencia – f / *incongruity* Lacking meaning or logic.

indigenismo americano – m / *American indigenous-native language* Hundreds of indigenous words from the Americas have been incorporated into the Spanish language since the time of the Discovery, especially from the nahua (spoken by the Aztecs), the quechua (spoken by the Incas), the aymara (spoken in the Andean region), the guaraní (spoken in the Paraná-

Paraguay basin), and the arahuaco and caribe (spoken in the Caribbean). Examples of some of these words are: cacique (Indian chief), tabaco (tobacco), tiza (chalk), tiburón (shark), cacahuete (peanut). (See also: americanismo)

indoeuropeo – adj / *Indo-European* Said of each of the languages deriving from a common origin and extending from India to Western Europe, including Spanish, Greek, Latin, English, German, Dutch, Russian, Polish, and outside of Europe, Persian, among others.

infijo – m / *infix* An affix inserted inside a word, and more specifically, inside a root or stem. Example: "hume(an)te" (smoking).

informal – adj / *informal* Refers to the form of address in Spanish indicated by the endings of the second person singular or the second person plural of all verbs in all moods and tenses. For example, in the present tense indicative of "cantar" (to sing), "cantas" (you sing, singular) and "cantáis" (you sing, plural). It is also called "the familiar form." (See also: formal)

intensidad – m / *intensity* The degree of force used in emiting or letting out the voice.

interdental – adj / *interdental* (See: punto de articulación)

interjección – f / *interjection* A word that expresses deep emotions, such as amazement, pain, love, surprise, etc. It has no specific function within a sentence, but it is added to highlight such emotions.

Some common Spanish interjections are: ¡Ay! ¡Eh! ¡Ojalá! ¡Caramba! ¡Ya! ¡Uf! Interjections can also be a group of words, like: ¡Dios mío! ¡Pues sí! ¡No me digas! and there are many others that, having a different grammatical value, are often used as interjections, like: ¡Silencio! ¡Adelante! ¡Hombre! etc. There are cases in which interjections form a complete sentence, like: ¡Oh Dios mío, cuánto sufrió esa familia! (Oh, God, how much did that family suffer!) Identical interjections can denote or convey different feelings ("¡oh!" may imply sorrow, amazement, or extreme happiness). There are also what are called "interjecciones propias" (proper or typical interjections), that is, always used as interjections, like: "¡Ay!" (Ow! Ouch!), and "interjecciones impropias" (improper or atypical interjections), like: ¡Silencio! (Silence!), ¡Hombre! (Man!). Some common Spanish interjections are:

¡Ay!	Ow! Ouch!
¡Eh!	Hey!
¡Oh!	Oh!
¡Ojalá!	I wish!
¡Ojo!	Watch out!
¡Caramba!	Good heavens!
¡Ya!	Enough!
¡Uf!	Whew! Yuk!

intervocálico – adj / *intervocalic* A consonant between two vowels, as the *h* in "ahora" (now), or the *z* in "azúcar" (sugar).

invariable – adj / *invariable* Something that doesn't change in any way, such as adverbs, past participles, and prepositions.

isosilábico – adj / *isosyllabic* Two or more words (or verse) having the same number of syllables. Example: bueno (good), luego (later).

italianismo – m / *Italianism* The use of an Italian word in another language. Example in Spanish: ópera, novela (novel), soneto (sonnet).

J

jerga – f/ argot – m / *slang* Just like in all other countries and languages, every Hispanic country uses slang. Here are some phrases:

jerga (country)	meaning
gilipollas (Spain)	jerk
guita (Argentina)	money
mi socio/mi sangre (Cuba)	my friend/my buddy
galleta (Cuba)	a slap on the face
cuate (Mexico)	pal
chueco (Mexico)	crooked
gringo (most Spanish-speaking countries)	national of the United States
gallego (most Spanish-speaking countries)	national of Spain
güero (Mexico)	person of fair complexion
guagua (Caribbean countries)	bus
guagua (South and Central America)	baby
camión (Central America)	bus
¡Vete a freír espárragos! (Spain)	Go to hell!
Darle la patá a la lata/ cantar el manicero (Cuba)	to die

Botar la pelota (Caribbean)	to do something great/outstanding
Estar como Carmelina (Cuba)	to be in good shape
Coger los mangos bajitos (Cuba, Caribbean)	to get a bargain, or to come out ahead in something

Like with any other language, Spanish has a variety of expletive words used mainly as interjections that vary depending on the country or region. Some of the most common are "¡coño!" and "¡carajo!" meaning "damn!" ("coño" also means "vagina" in Spain), and "¡mierda!" meaning "shit!" There are also words with double meaning that should be avoided, like "coger," meaning "to have intercourse" in many South American countries, and "papaya," which besides the fruit means a woman's vagina in most Caribbean countries.

jerigonza – f / *secret code or language* Complicated and difficult to understand language proper of some unions, trades, and criminal societies.

judeoespañol – **adj** / *Judeo-Spanish* Name belonging to or relative to the Sephardim and the peculiar kind of Spanish they speak, principally in Asia Minor, the Balkans, and North Africa, which preserves almost intact many of the characteristics of the Spanish spoken before the sixteenth century. "Sephardic" in Hebrew means "Spanish" or "Spaniard." Many of the Jews who settled in the United States in the nineteenth century were Sephardic Jews.

L

labiodental – adj / *labiodental* (See: punto de articulación)

ladino – m / *Ladino* A kind of Spanish or Spanish dialect spoken by the Jews in medieval Spain, which is now spoken by Sephardim in the Orient. It is a mix of Hebrew and old Spanish.

laísmo – m (Peculiar to Spanish, no English translation) Irregular usage of the forms "la" and "las" of the pronoun "ella" for the indirect object. Example: La traigo un regalo para su cumpleaños. (instead of Le traigo un regalo para su cumpleaños.) (I bring her a gift for her birthday.)

latinismo – m / *Latinism* Expression or manner of speaking proper of the Latin language. For example, "ad hoc," literally meaning "for this," and "honoris causa," literally meaning "due to reason or cause."

latino – adj / *Latin* Used also as a noun. Term loosely used in the United States to refer to a person of Hispanic descent, or to a Spanish-speaking person. According to the Royal Spanish Academy, it refers to a native of any of the countries of Europe or America speaking a language derived from Latin. Based on this definition, a French person, a Spaniard, a Portuguese, and a Canadian could also be called "latinos," when in fact they would not be considered as such in the United States. Other terms loosely used in the United States with the same connotation are "Hispanic," "Hispanic-American," and at one time "Spanish-American," with the understanding that "America" is the United States. The term "Hispanic" leaves out both Portugal and Brazil, as well as all of the indigenous people of the Americas, as does "latino." Also, the term "Ibero-American" has been used, and although it does include Portugal and Brazil, it leaves out all of the indigenous people. To add to the confusion, "America" is an Italian name < "Americus" used by mistake by a German map maker. As for "latinoamericano" (Latin-American), based on the definition by the Royal Academy of the Language, the term would also apply to the Canadians, or at least to the French-speaking Canadians of the province of Quebec and to many of those who settled in the United States during the eighteenth century as far south as Alabama and Louisiana. Based on the above, there is not a single term that would be applicable to the Spanish-speaking region of the Americas other than "Americano," which would also be used to distinguish the one to the North from the one to the South: "North Americans" and "South Americans," as it is done in Spanish ("norteamericanos" and "sudamericanos"), and also "Central Americans" ("centroamericanos").

leísmo – m / (Peculiar to Spanish, no English translation) Incorrect use of the direct or indirect object pronouns "le" and "les" when referring to things instead of persons. For example, when you say, referring to a newspaper: Le compré en la tienda. (I bought it in the store.) instead of the correct Lo compré en la tienda.

lengua – f / idioma – m / lenguaje – m / *language* Generally, the communication of thoughts and feelings by means of vocal sounds to which meaning is attributed; human speech. Also, the body and manner of speech of every nation, e.g., Spanish, Arabic, Russian.

lengua castellana – f / *Castilian (Spanish) language* (See: castellano)

lengua clásica – f / *classical language* That which reached a perfect or near-perfect degree of development and excellence, and left works that have served as models, such as Latin and Greek.

lengua culta – f / *learned language* That which is spoken by learned people concerned with the correct use of the oral and written language.

lengua escrita – f / *written language* Letter, document, or any manuscript, typed, or printed paper.

lengua española – f / *Spanish language* Derived from Latin and belonging to the Romance/Neo-latin Languages. It was declared an official language in the thirteenth century under the reign of Alfonso X "the Wise." It has been influenced by many languages, including Arabic, French, and present-day English, as well as by some of the indigenous languages of the Americas.

lengua extranjera – f / *foreign language* A language spoken in a foreign country.

lengua flexional – f / *flexional-flectional language* The one modifying words by their endings, or by inflection, like Spanish.

lengua franca – f / *lingua franca* That which is a mix of two or more languages and is understood by natives of different countries. Such was precisely the intent of the creators of Esperanto, but with little success. French is a lingua franca in North Africa, as is Portuguese in certain parts of Africa, and Tagalog in the Philippines. We may also refer to Spanish as a lingua franca in Central and South America (with the exception of Brazil, where Portuguese may also be considered a lingua franca), and Quechua, spoken manly in Peru, but also in parts of Bolivia, Ecuador, Colombia, Argentina, and Chile.

lengua hablada – f / *spoken language* That which is expressed through the spoken word.

lengua materna – f / *mother language* What Spanish is or represents for any Hispanic country, and English for the United States or any other English-speaking country, such as Australia or New Zealand. Also Latin with respect to Spanish or French.

lengua monosilábica – f / *monosyllabic language* The one using words consisting of only one syllable, such as Chinese.

lengua mozárabe – f / *Mozarabic language* It refers to the now extinct Romance language, derived from the Vulgar Latin spoken by the Visigoths and influenced by Arabic. The Mozarabic language was spoken by Christians and Moors in Spain during the Islamic dominion from the eighth to the fifteenth century.

lengua muerta – f / *extinct language* The one that was spoken in ancient times in any country or nation, such as Sanskrit.

lengua neolatina – f / *neo-Latin language* A language originated or derived from Latin. (See also: lengua romance)

lengua oral – f / *oral language* The spoken language.

lengua popular – f / *popular language* The language commonly spoken in any country

lengua romance – f / *Romance language* A language derived from Latin, such as Spanish, French, Italian, or Portuguese.

lengua santa – f / *sacred/holy language* Hebrew, because it was the language in which the Holy Scriptures were written, and Aramaic, because it was spoken in Palestine in the time of Jesus Christ.

lengua vulgar – f / *common language* It refers mainly to the language spoken under Roman rule, like Latin in Spain.

lenguaje – m / *language* The means by which people express their ideas and sensations.

lenguaje coloquial – m / *colloquial language*
Language that is informal in conversation or writing, but not necessarily substandard or illiterate. Many famous Spanish and Latin American writers have used colloquial language in their writings, such as Pío Baroja, from Spain, or Carlos Fuentes, from Mexico.

lenguaje figurado – m / *figurative language*
Language using rhetorical figures. The most common figures of speech are metaphor and simile. (See: metáfora and símil)

lenguaje profano– m / *profane language* Language that shows disrespect or irreverence toward God or sacred/holy things.

lenguaje soez – m / *low/rude/coarse language*
Lacking grace, tact, taste, etc.

letra – f / *letter* Any of the graphic symbols or characters that constitute the alphabet of a language. In Spanish, for example, *a, ch, m, t, x.*

letra cursiva – f / *italics* Also called "letra bastardilla" or "letra itálica." Example: *Don Quijote de la Mancha.*

letra de imprenta/de molde – f / *print letter*
Writing letters resembling those printed in type, as opposed to script or any other writing style. Example: N, T, Z.

letra mayúscula – f / *capital/uppercase letter*
Most rules governing the use of capital letters in Spanish are identical to the rules controlling Eng-

lish. Some rules that are typical of Spanish are: When double letters start a sentence, only the first one is capitalized, e.g., *Ch*, *Ll*. The orthographical accent is also used over capital letters, as in "AMÉRICA." In titles, only the first word is capitalized: Gerente general de ventas (General Sales Manager).

letra minúscula – **f** / *lowercase letter* The type of letter constantly used in writing.

letra negrita – **f** / *boldface/bold type letter* In printing, any type with a heavy face. As an example, all entries in this dictionary are listed in boldface.

letra versalita – **f** / *small capital letter* Any letter of the alphabet written in small capitals. Example: SEVILLA.

léxico – **m** / *lexicon/vocabulary* The complete dictionary of a language, or the total of words that make up a language.

lexicografía – **f** / *lexicography* The part of linguistics dealing with the theoretical principles on which the editing and general work of dictionaries is based.

lingüística – **f** / *linguistics* The comparative and philosophical study of languages.

lítotes/litotes – **f** / *litotes* Figure in rhetoric consisting of not expressing all that is meant to be conveyed. It is generally used to negate the opposite of what is affirmed. Examples: Ella no es tan insentata. (She's not as foolish.); No fue mucho lo que discutieron. (It wasn't much what they discussed.) It is also called "atenuación" in Spanish.

locución – f / *locution/phrase* A meaningful group of words.

locución adjetiva – f / *adjectival phrase* The one acting as an adjective. For example, "de rechupete" (delicious, referring manily to food).

locución adverbial – f / *adverbial phrase* The one acting as an adverb. Example: de pronto (suddenly). Other common adverbial phrases are: por si acaso (just in case), en el acto (right away), de arriba abajo (from top to bottom), por ahora (for now), a la antigua (the old-fashioned way), a brazo partido (all the way), a ciegas (blindly), a toda costa (at all costs), cara a cara (face to face), a gusto (to taste), hoy por hoy (at this moment in time), a la larga (in the long run), en lugar de (instead of), a mano (by hand), a la moda (in fashion), de palabra en palabra (word by word), apenas (hardly).

locución conjuntiva – f / *conjunctive phrase* The one acting as a conjunction. Example: con tal de que (provided that).

locución preposicional – f / *prepositional phrase* The one acting as a preposition. Example: alrededor de (around).

locución pronominal – f / *pronominal phrase* The one acting as a pronoun. Example: alguna que otra (one or another).

locución sustantiva – f / *substantive phrase* The one acting as a noun. Example: el otro mundo (the other world).

locución verbal – f / *verbal phrase* The one acting as a verb. Example: caerse de rodillas (to fall on one's knees).

loísmo – m / (Peculiar to Spanish, no English translation.) Error consisting of using the forms "lo" and "los" of the pronoun "él" as an indirect object when referring to masculine nouns. Example: Los encontramos durmiendo. (We found them sleeping.) instead of Les encontramos durmiendo.

M

masculino – adj / *masculine* Refers to one of the two genders in Spanish, usually nouns ending in *o*, like "amigo" (male friend), "libro" (book), "viento" (wind). There are exceptions, however, like "la mano" (the hand).

medio – m-adj-adv / *middle-half* This word can have three different functions within a sentence. It can be an adjective, as in "medio pasaje" (half fare/half price), an adverb, as in "Juan está medio dormido." (John is half asleep.), and a noun, as in "en el medio del pueblo" (in the middle of the town). The only "medio" changing in gender and number is the adjective, thus it is incorrect to say "Emilia está media dormida." instead of "Emilia está medio dormida." because "medio" in this case is an adverb.

metáfora – f / *metaphor* A figure of speech in which a word or a phrase that usually designates one thing is used to designate another. For example: Tomás es un león. (Thomas is a lion.), meaning that he is very strong. Note these metaphors by the Spanish poet Federico García Lorca: "labios de cielo" (heavenly lips), meaning "sweet and passionate lips," and "ojos como dardos" (eyes like darts), meaning "piercing eyes."

metátesis – f / *metathesis* The transposition of a letter or sound in a word. Example: "cocreta" for "croqueta" (croquette).

metonimia – f / *metonymy* The use of the name of one thing for that of another. Example: Murió a hierro. (He/she died of stab wounds.) to say Murió a cuchilladas.

modal – adj / *modal* Belonging or relative to the grammatical mood.

modismo – m / *idiom* Refers to a phrase that is peculiar to a particular language, and in which the meaning of the words used together as a group is different from their literal individual meaning. In the Spanish idiom "hombre de pelo en pecho" (a brave man), the literal meaning of "pelo" is hair, and of "pecho" chest. However, when combined together in that idiom they lose their literal meaning and convey something else. Contrary to common belief, idioms are not, and should not be confused with, adverbial phrases, like, for example, "a pesar de" (in spite of), "de vez en cuando" (once in a while).

modo – m / *mood* A category in grammar expressed through inflection. There are four moods (three, for some, counting the conditional as part of the indicative) in Spanish: indicativo (indicative), imperativo (imperative or command), potencial (conditional), subjuntivo (subjunctive).

modo de articulación – m / *manner of articulation* The special disposition of the speech organs in the pronunciation of consonant sounds, classified in the following groups:

africada (affricate) pronounced by combining a stop and a fricate, or when slowly released consonants are immediately followed by fricatives at the same place of articulation, like the *ch* in "ocho" (eight)

fricativa (fricative) pronounced by forcing the air through a narrow opening between the lips and the teeth, like during pronunciation of the letter *b* in "lobo" (wolf)

oclusiva (occlusive) pronounced preventing temporarily the passage of air or breath, like the letter *p* in "limpio" (clean)

The five vowels in Spanish also belong to this group; they are pronounced by an opening of the speech organs sufficiently wide to allow the air to flow out uninterruptedly. The opening varies according to the pronunciation of each vowel. Also belonging to this group is the nasal sound produced through the nose, like the Spanish *ñ* in "niña" (girl), and the "sonora" (voiced) and "sorda" (voiceless) sounds (see each one separately).

modo imperativo – m / *command mood*
Expresses a command or request. It has only one tense, the present, and lacks a first person singular ("I") form. The only true command forms are the second singular and the second plural, because the

other three are taken from the subjunctive mood. The command mood may be affirmative or negative (with different verb endings), and many of its verbs are irregular. Example of a command conjugation in the affirmative and the negative using the *AR* regular verb "hablar" (to speak):

affirmative	negative
¡Habla! (Speak!)	¡No hables! (Don't speak!, informal singular)
¡Hable! (Speak!)	¡No hable! (Don't speak!, formal singular)
¡Hablemos! (Let's speak!)	¡No hablemos! (Let us not speak!)
¡Hablad! (Speak!)	¡No habléis! (Don't speak!, informal plural)
¡Hablen! (Speak!)	¡No hablen! (Don't speak!, formal and also informal plural in most Hispanic countries)

As it can be seen, English has only one form, "Speak!" whereas Spanish has five: two informal in the singular and plural, and two formal in the singular and plural, plus the "we" form. In other words, when we say in English "Speak!" it can be anybody in the singular or plural, making no distinction about who the person is. We also see that

in the affirmative the first singular ("Habla") and
the second plural ("Hablad") are the true command
forms, whereas the others ("Hable," "Hablemos,"
and "Hablen") are subjunctive forms. On the other
hand, all of the negative forms are taken from the
subjunctive. Some of the irregular command verbs
in Spanish are: tener (to have), ir (to go), venir (to
come), poner (to put), hacer (to do/make), decir (to
say/tell). Here are some examples using the singular informal affirmative command of these verbs:

¡Ten cuidado!	Be careful!
¡Ve a casa de Pedro!	Go to Peter's house!
¡Ven enseguida!	Come right away!
¡Ponte el abrigo!	Put on your coat!
¡Haz la tarea!	Do your home-work!
¡Di la verdad!	Tell/say the truth!

modo indicativo – m / *indicative mood* It
expresses an act, state, or happening as actual or
factual, as distinguished from the conditional and
the subjunctive. In other words, it is used to state
facts: what really is and happens. The indicative
has a total of eight tenses in Spanish, four simple
and four compound. In the following example, we
are using the regular *AR* verb "trabajar" (to work)
in the first person singular.

simple	**example**
presente (present)	trabajo (I work)
pretérito indefinido (preterit)	trabajé (I worked)

| **pretérito imperfecto** (imperfect) | trabajaba (I worked/used to work) |
| **futuro imperfecto** (future) | trabajaré (I will/shall work) |

compound	**example**
pretérito perfecto (present perfect)	he trabajado (I have worked)
pretérito pluscuamperfecto (past perfect/pluperfect)	había trabajado (I had worked)
pretérito anterior* (past perfect)	hube trabajado (I had worked)
futuro perfecto (future perfect)	habré trabajado (I will/shall have worked)

*The difference between the "pretérito anterior" and the "pretérito pluscuamperfecto" (both expressing a past action taking place before another past action) is that one denotes the past action as being immediate, while the other is farther into the past. Example of the first: Tan pronto hubo llamado José, se fueron a trabajar. (As soon as Joseph had called they left for work.) Example of the second: Vieron a la mujer que habían conocido en Venezuela. (They saw the woman they had met in Venezuela.) The present perfect denotes a past action close to the present, and the future perfect denotes a future action taking place before another future action. Example of the first: He abierto la ventana. (I have opened the window.) Example of the second: Cuando llegues ya habré comido. (I will have already eaten by the time you arrive.)

modo potencial – m / *conditional mood* It has two tenses, the "potencial simple" (simple conditional) and the "potencial compuesto" (conditional perfect). In independent sentences using one verb, the conditional simple means possibility, as in: Me gustaría hablar con él otra vez. (I would like to talk to him again.), and in conditional sentences, such as: Si pudiéramos, saldríamos más temprano. (If we could, we would leave earlier.) The conditional perfect expresses a future action in relation to the past, although that future action is prior to another action. It is formed with the conditional of the auxiliary verb "haber" (to have, which is irregular) plus a past participle, as in: Nos dijeron que cuando nos reuniéramos habrían terminado. (They told us that by the time we got together, they would have finished.)

modo subjuntivo – m / *subjunctive mood*
Expresses actions seen as doubtful, possible, needed, or desired, as opposed to the indicative mood, which expresses what is factual and definite. In Spanish, the subjunctive is more often used in subordinate or dependent clauses, all introduced by the key word "que." The most typical Spanish subjunctive sentence actually uses two sentences (a main sentence and a dependent one), two subjects, two verbs, with each sentence linked by "que." The subjunctive will always appear in the subordinate or dependent clause, following verbs that express doubt, hope, need, possibility, or desire, used in the indicative mood. Regarding irregular verbs, if the verb is irregular in the first person singular of the present indicative, it will also be irregular in all six forms of the present subjunctive. Example using the verb "hacer" (to do/make):

present indicative	present subjunctive
hago	haga
haces	hagas
hace	haga
hacemos	hagamos
hacéis	hagáis
hacen	hagan

And, usually, if the verb in the main clause is in the present or future tense, the subjunctive in the subordinate clause will be in the present tense, and if it is in the preterit or imperfect in the main clause, then it will be in the imperfect subjunctive in the subordinate clause. Examples:

main clause		subordinate clause
Espero	que	vengas.
Esperaba	que	vinieras/vinieses.

The aforementioned examples also show the typical use of "que" in the typical Spanish subjunctive sentence, as mentioned earlier.

The subjunctive can also be used with impersonal expressions denoting volition or desire:

Spanish	English
Es importante que estudies.	It is important that you study.
Es necesario que lo llames.	It is necessary for you to call him.
Ojalá que pases el curso.	I hope/it is hoped that you pass the course.

It may also be used with certain expressions, such as:

para que

Los voy a llamar para que vengan.	I am going to call them so that they can come.

a menos que

No podré ir a menos que vaya con María.	I won't be able to go unless I go with Mary.

con tal (de) que

Sí lo puedo hacer con tal de que me ayudes.	Yes, I can do it, provided you help me.

It is never easy to translate the Spanish subjunctive into English, simply because English doesn't have specific subjunctive tenses as Spanish does. There are a total of four subjunctive tenses in Spanish, two simple and two compound or perfect. There are also the future and future perfect tenses, but they are rarely used today. The imperfect subjunctive has two endings in Spanish, either one being correct. Example: The verb "caminar" (to walk) in the various tenses of the subjunctive:

presente	pretérito imperfecto
camine	caminara/caminase
camines	caminaras/caminases
camine	caminara/caminase
caminemos	camináramos/caminásemos
caminéis	caminarais/caminaseis
caminen	caminaran/caminasen

pretérito perfecto	pretérito pluscuamperfecto
haya caminado	hubiera/hubiese caminado
hayas caminado	hubieras/hubieses caminado
haya caminado	hubiera/hubiese caminado
hayamos caminado	hubiéramos/hubiésemos caminado
hayáis caminado	hubierais/hubieseis caminado
hayan caminado	hubieran/hubiesen caminado

Generally, the present perfect subjunctive uses the present perfect indicative in Spanish, and the past perfect subjunctive in English. Examples:

Spanish	English
Dudo que hayan venido.	I doubt that they have come.

monolingüe – adj / *monolingual* Speaking only one language.

monosemia – f / *monosemy* Refers to words having a single meaning, such as: nariz (nose), claridad (clarity), as opposed to "polisemia" (see).

monosílabo – adj / *monosyllable* A word having one syllable. Example: sol (sun), flor (flower).

morfema – m / *morpheme* The smallest linguistic unit of a language with semantic meaning. For example, in the word "untouchable" there are three morphemes: "un," "touch," and "able." The only one that can stand alone is "touch" while the other two, "un" and "able," one a prefix and the other a suffix, are dependent on another word. Thus, "touch" is a free morpheme, and "un" and "able" are bound morphemes.

morfología – f / *morphology* The part of grammar that deals with how words are structured.

múltiplo – adj / *multiple* Said of a numeral noun or adjective, whose meaning is determined by the multiplication of an amount. Example: veces (times).

mutación ortográfica – f / *orthographical mutation* Refers to verbs that are not considered irregular even though they alter some of their letters in order to conform to orthographical changes. Thus, not irregular are those changing the *c* to *z* or *qu*; those changing the *z* or *qu* to *c*; those changing the *g* to *gu* or *j*; those ending in *guir*, eliminating the *u* before *a* or *o* (like in "distinguir" > "distingo/a"); those ending in *uir*, changing the *i* to *y*, like the verb "oír," among others.

c to *qu*	masques < mascar (to chew)
g to *gu*	lleguemos < llegar (to arrive)
guir to *go*	sigo < seguir (to follow)
uir to *y*	huyo < huir (to flee)
oír	oyó < oír (he/she heard)

muy – adv / *very* Apocopated form of "mucho" when preceding an adjective or another adverb. Example: muy bueno (very good), muy tarde (very late).

N

nasal – adj / *nasal* (See: modo de articulación)

negativo – adj / *negative* (See: afirmativo)

neologismo – m / *neologism* A new word, meaning, or expression in a language. Examples: correo electrónico (e-mail), bolsa de aire (air bag), acupuntura (acupuncture).

neutro – adj / *neuter* In Spanish, there are no neuter forms for any noun, nor are there neuter forms for the inflection of the adjective. Only the article, the personal pronoun of the third person, the demonstratives, and some pronouns have neuter forms that differentiate in the singular. "Ello" and "lo" are neuter pronouns, as in: No hay dinero, pero no te preocupes por ello. (There is no money, but don't worry about it.); No te di las gracias, lo siento. (I didn't thank you, I am sorry about it.) "Lo" is also a neuter article that is mostly used with singular abstract substantive adjectives, as in: lo bello, lo bueno. There are cases, however, in which it can precede pural adjectives, as in: ¡Lo bandidos que son esos tipos! (What crooks those guys are!), and feminine adjectives, as in: Me quedé asombrado de lo fea que era esa casa. (I was amazed at how ugly that house was.) The neuter "esto" is a demonstrative pronoun, as in: No me gusta esto. (I don't like this.)

nexo – m / *nexus* A tie, link, or connection.

nombre – m / *name-noun* Word designating or identifying animate or inaminate beings. Example: niño (child), árbol (tree), Roma (Rome), envidia (envy). Which is correct, "nombre" or "sustantivo"? It all depends: "nombre" is "name" and "sustantivo" or "nombre sustantivo" is "noun." In grammar, "sustantivo" or "nombre sustantivo" is generally used.

nombre abstracto – m / *abstract noun* The noun naming ideas, characteristics, or intangible qualities. Examples: cariño (love), valentía (courage), amistad (friendship), pesar (sorrow).

nombre apelativo – m / *noun* The noun that designates persons or animals: Tomás (Thomas), Cristóbal (Christopher), Coco (coconut, for a white dog).

nombre colectivo – m / *collective noun* The noun that, being singular, expresses a group of persons, animals, or things: batallón (battalion), la gente (people), enjambre (swarm).

nombre común – m / *common noun* The noun applied to persons, animals, or objects that belong to the same class or species: manzana (apple), caballo (horse).

nombre concreto – m / *concrete noun* The noun naming tangible things. Example: lluvia (rain), nube (cloud), libro (book).

nombre despectivo – m / *disparaging noun* A noun denoting contempt by the addition of a suffix. Example: villorrio (shantytown), cabezotas (big head), amigote (bad friend), populacho (masses, also plebs, mob), reyezuelo (kinglet), pajarraco (ugly bird).

nombre numeral – m / *numeral noun* The noun that referes to numbers, such as: docena (dozen), millar (thousand).

nombre partitivo – m / *partitive noun* The noun that restricts or pertains only to a part of a whole. Example: diezmo (tithe).

nombre patronímico – m / *patronymic noun* A surname derived from the name of the parents by the addition of a prefix or suffix. In Spanish: "Hernández" from "Hernando," "González" from "Gonzalo." The patronymic suffix is *ez*, meaning "son of." An example in English would be "Stevenson" from "Steven," or "Robertson" from "Robert."

nombre propio – m / *proper noun* The noun applied to animated or inanimated beings: persons, animals, or things, such as "Miguel" (Michael), Barcelona.

nombre sustantivo A word that can function as the subject of a sentence, such as: el mar (the sea), la peluquera (the hairdresser), María Isabel. (See also: nombre)

nomenclatura – f / *nomenclature* Lexicon of technical words. Example: Nomenclatura jurídica (Legal Nomenclature).

nominal – adj / *nominal* Belonging to or relating to a noun.

norma – f / *norm* One of the grammatical principles that regulate the correct usage of a language.

número – m / *number* Refers to nouns that can be either singular or plural: la flor (the flower), los cuadros (the paintings).

número cardinal – m / *cardinal number* "Uno, dos, tres," etc. (one, two, three, etc.). In Spanish, from the number 16 to 29, one or two words can be used, as in: diez y siete or diecisiete (seventeen), veinte y cuatro or veinticuatro (twenty- four). "Ciento," a noun, is used before other numbers, like "doscientos" (two hundred), "seiscientos" (six hundred), whereas the adjective "cien" (a/one hundred), an apocopated form of "ciento," is used before nouns, as in: cien libros (a/one hundred books). Important note: In English, a comma is used to separate the thousands from the hundreds, as in: 1,200, whereas in most of the Spanish-speaking world a period is used, as in: 1.200. Also, generally, a "billion" in English is one thousand times a million, but in Spanish a "billón" is a million times a million, as the Latin prefix *bi* means "two" or "two times." However, in England, sometimes a "billion" has the same meaning as in Spanish.

número ordinal – m / *ordinal number* "Primero, segundo, tercero," etc. (first, second, third, etc.). Used as adjectives, ordinal numbers agree in gender and number with the noun, as in: lección primera (first lesson), capítulos primeros (first chapters). When "primero" and "tercero" precede a masculine singular noun, the *o* is dropped, as in: primer piso (first floor), primer día del mes (the first day of the month).

objeto – m / *object* (See: complemento directo and complemento indirecto)

obsoleto – adj / *obsolete-archaic* An antiquated word, phrase, grammatical construction, or expression, no longer in use. For example, "principesa" for "princesa" (princess), "no lo cantando" for "no cantándolo" (not singing it). (See also: arcaísmo)

oclusiva – adj / *occlusive* (See: modo de articulación)

onomatopeya – f / *onomatopoeia* An imitation through words of natural sounds. Example of animals: miau (meow), of things: tictac (tick-tock).

oración – f / *sentence* A word or group of words expressing something grammatically complete, usually containing a subject and a predicate. Example: Buenos Aires es la capital de Argentina. (Buenos Aires is the capital of Argentina.)

oración adjetiva/oración relativa – f / *adjectival sentence* Refers to a sentence in which a noun or pronoun of the main clause acts as an adjective or past participle. It is used in subordination with any of the relative pronouns "que, quien, cual, cuyo." Example: El hombre que trabaja, tendrá su recompensa. (The man who works will be rewarded.), which equals El hombre trabajador será recompensado. (The working man will be compensated.)

oración adversativa – f / *adversative sentence*
That which contradicts or restricts its meaning, contrasting a negative with an affirmative. Example: El canalla mudará su sonrisa, pero no su conciencia. (The swine may change his smile, but not his conscience.)

oración atributiva – f / *attributive sentence* A simple sentence with a predicate formed by a copulative verb (such as "ser" or "estar") plus a complement or attribute. Example: El marido de mi hermana es dentista. (My sister's husband is a dentist.)

oración compuesta – f / *compound sentence*
The one that is formed by two simple sentences joined grammatically. Examples: Eduardo y Carlos van a la universidad. (Edward and Charles go to college.); Mi maestro es inteligente y comprensivo. (My teacher is intelligent and understanding.) The first sentence has two subjects and the second has two predicates.

oración condicional – f / *conditional sentence*
A sentence that is subject to, implying, or depending upon a condition. It is used generally with the conjunction "si" (if), but also with some others like "siempre que" (provided that), "ya que" (since), etc. Example: Si no hablas con Jaime, te vas a meter en un lío. (If you don't talk to James, you're going to get in trouble.)

oración coordinada – f / *coordinate sentence*
That which is connected to another by a conjunction. Example: La belleza en una mujer se hallará

en su alma y no en su figura. (Beauty in a woman will be found in her soul, not in her looks.) This kind of sentence may also be connected by juxtaposition (omitting the conjunction), as in: Me levanto, me visto, salgo, corro a trabajar. (I get up, get dressed, leave, run to work.)

oración copulativa – f / *copulative sentence*
This is a coordinate sentence (see: oración coordinada) in which the connector is the copulative conjunction "e/y" or "ni" (and, or). Examples: Madre e hija son costureras. (Mother and daughter are seamtresses.); El hombre propone y Dios dispone. (Man proposes and God disposes.)

oración disyuntiva – f / *disjunctive sentence* A sentence expressing the incompatibility of two or more predicates of the same subject. Example: O haces la cama o esta noche no duermes. (Either you make the bed or tonight you won't sleep.) The conjunction "o," when preceding a word beginning with another "o," changes to "u," as in: "plata u oro" (silver or gold). Also, when the conjunction "y" (and) is used, and it precedes a word beginning with *i*, the "y" changes to "e," as in "…e interrumpió la conversación" (…and interrupted the conversation).

oración exclamativa – f / *exclamative sentence*
That which expresses an emotion, such as affection, love, happiness, pain, etc. Example: ¡Cuánto me alegro que estés bien! (I am very happy that you are well!)

oración enunciativa – m / *enunciative sentence* That which expresses a fact, a thought, or an action in the affirmative or the negative, as in: Él es muy alto. (He's very tall.); Ella no hizo la tarea. (She didn't do the homework.)

oración impersonal – f / *impersonal sentence* An impersonal sentence is generally expressed by way of a verb in the third person plural. Example: Le despidieron del trabajo. (They fired him from his job.) If the verb is not in the third person plural, it is formed by "se" plus the verb in the third person singular. Example: Se llamó a los testigos. (The witnesses were called.)

oración predicativa – f / *predicative sentence* A simple sentence that uses a non-copulative verb (such as "ser" or "estar") as the nucleus of the predicate, as in: Llegó cansado. (He arrived tired.)

oración nominal – f / *nominal sentence* That lacking a verb. Example: año de cosecha (harvest year).

oración simple – f / *simple sentence* The one using only one predicate. Example: Miguel trabaja en Bogotá. (Michael works in Bogota.)

oración subordinada – f / *subordinate sentence* In a compound sentence, the part depending on the main part. Example: Voy contigo al cine si me pagas la entrada. (I'll go with you to the movies if you pay for it.)

oración subordinada sustantiva – f / *substantive subordinate sentence* That which corresponds to a noun, a nominal syntagm, or a pronoun. They could be substituted by a pronoun: Quiere que se lo compres. (He/she wants you to buy it for him/her.); Queremos eso./Lo queremos. (We want that./We want it.), and be introduced by such links as the conjunctions "que" and "si": Nos parece bien que le des el dinero. (We think it is a good idea for you to give him/her the money.), or a pronoun or an interrogative pronoun: Se negó a decirme cómo lo había hecho. (He/she refused to tell me how he/she did it.), or not be introduced by any links: No quería saberlo. (I didn't want to know it.)

oración unipersonal – **f** / *unipersonal sentence* Formed with verbs expressing atmospheric phenomena and used in the third person singular of any tense, such as "llover" (to rain), "nevar" (to snow), "tronar" (to thunder), etc. Example: En Puerto Rico llueve mucho. (In Puerto Rico it rains a lot.)

oración yuxtapuesta – **f** / *juxtaposed sentence* One not requiring conjunctions in coordinate or subordinate sentences. Example: Era de madrugada, aún no había salido el sol. (It was dawn; the sun had not yet come out.)

oral – **adj** / *oral* That which is manifested or produced with the mouth or through the spoken word.

oratoria – **f** / *oratory* The art of speaking with eloquence.

órganos de articulación – **m, pl** / *organs of articulation* The principal organs of articulation are:

Spanish	English
la cavidad nasal	nasal cavity
el alvéolo	alveolus
la nariz	nose
los labios	lips
los dientes	teeth
el ápice de la lengua	tip of the tongue or apex
el predorso de la lengua	tongue blade
el postdorso de la lengua	tongue back
la glotis	glottis
la epiglotis	epiglottis
la laringe	larynx
los bronquios	bronchial tubes
la tráquea	trachea/windpipe
los pulmones	lungs
las cuerdas vocals	vocal cords or folds
la cavidad faríngea	pharyngeal cavity
la úvula	uvula
el paladar blando/ el velo del paladar	soft palate or velum
el paladar duro	hard palate
la cavidad oral	oral cavity

ortografía – f / *orthography/spelling* Deals with the correct use of letters, accentuation (primarily the written accent), and all the signs and symbols of the written language.

ortología – f / *orthology* Deals with the correct pronunciation and use of a language.

oxímoron – m / *oxymoron* In rhetoric, the combination of two adjoining words with opposite meanings. Example: Una calma aterradora. (A terrifying calm.)

oxítona – adj / *oxytone* A word carrying the accent on the last syllable. For example, "pared" (wall), "familiar" (relative).

P

palabra – f / *word* The graphic representation of the spoken word.

palabra compuesta – f / *compound word* That formed by two or more words; for example, "paraguas" (umbrella), "hispanomericano" (Hispanic-American), "pelirrojo" (red-haired).

palabrería – f / *chatter* Meaningless talk.

palabrota – f / *swearword* (See: improperio)

palatal – adj / *palatal* (See: punto de articulación)

paradigma – m / *paradigm* That which serves as a model or pattern. A set of all inflection forms of any given word, such as a noun or verb; for example, the paradigm of a regular verb.

paradoja – f / *paradox* Figure consisting in using contradictory expressions or phrases. Example: Mira al pobre, en su miseria rico. (Look at the poor man, in his misery, rich.)

paráfrasis – f / *paraphrase* A restatement or rewording of a text or passage, usually for the purpose of clarification.

paragoge – m / *paragoge* The addition of a letter or syllable at the end of a word. For example, "huéspede" for "huésped" (guest).

parasíntesis – f / *parasynthesis* The forming of words by composition and derivation; in other words, words that are formed by adding a prefix and suffix. Examples: endulzar < en + dulce + ar (to sweeten), pordiosero < por + dios + ero (beggar).

parasintético – adj / *parasynthetic* (See: parasíntesis)

parataxis – f / *parataxis* Coordination or juxtaposition in a clause. (See: yuxtaposición)

paréntesis – m / *parenthesis* Used when the meaning of a sentence is interrupted to make a necessary explanation or clarification. Example: Me gustaría (aunque te moleste) que me ayudaras con este trabajo. (I would like you [although it may bother you] to help me with this job.)
A parentheseis may also be defined as an incidental sentence or phrase, not necessarily linked with the other members of the period, the meaning of which it interrupts but does not alter.
Often the dash is used instead of the parenthesis, as in: El problema fue—y fue un gran problema—que dejé la llave en casa. (The problem was—and it was a big problem—that I left the key at home.)
Note that, in Spanish, the period is placed after the closing parenthesis >).

parentético – adj / *parenthetic/parenthetical* (See: paréntesis)

parónimo – adj / *paronym* Refers to words that are almost homonyms but are slightly different in pronunciation or spelling. For example, "especial" (spice), "especie" (species).

paronomasia – f / *paronomasia* In Spanish, similarity of two or more words that differ only in the stressed vowel. For example, "pelo" (hair) and "polo" (polo), "circo" (circus) and "cerco" (siege).

paroxítona – adj / *paroxytone* In Spanish, words that are stressed on the next to the last syllable. Also called "penúltima" (penult). For example, "amigo" (friend), "escuela" (school), "camino" (road).

párrafo – m / *paragraph* Each of the divisions in writing indicated by a capital letter at the beginning of a line or by a period at the end of a text.

parte de la oración – f / *part of speech* Each of the different kinds of words that make up a sentence, such as nouns, pronouns, verbs, adverbs, adjectives, etc. For example, in the sentence "La corbata es roja y amarilla." (The tie is red and yellow.), "la corbata" is a noun, "es" is a verb, and "roja" and "amarilla" are adjectives.

participio – m / *participle* A nonpersonal form of the verb that can change in gender and number, and that is often assimilated to the adjective in its grammatical function. For example, "cansado/a/os/as" (tired), "preocupado/a/os/as" (worried). It is often used with the verb "estar" (to be), as in: Estoy cansado. (I am tired.)

participio pasado – m / *past participle* Also called "participio pasivo" (passive participle). In Spanish, past participles are used to form compound or perfect tenses along with the helping verb "haber." They are formed by adding the ending *ado* to *AR*-ending verbs, and *ido* to *ER*- and *IR*-ending verbs, but only in the case of regular verbs (which make up the majority of Spanish verbs). (See: tiempo compuesto) When the past participle is not used to form compound tenses, it functions merely as an adjective, in which case it agrees in gender and number with the noun. For example, "casa comprada" (bought house), "frutas vendidas" (sold fruits). In addition, past participles can also function as nouns; for example, "la ida y la vuelta" (going and returning); "Esta es la entrada y esa la salida." (This is the entrance and that is the exit.) Also, some verbs have both regular and irregular past participles, although usually the irregular ones function mainly as adjectives, for example, "confundido" and "confuso," "bendecido," and "bendito," as in:

Han confundido los números.	They have confused the numbers.
Ese libro es muy confuso.	That book is very confusing.

Usually, the irregular past participles end in *to, so,* and *cho,* as in: vuelto, expreso, hecho. Some of the common verbs with irregular past participles are: hecho (from "hacer," to do or to make), escrito (from "escribir," to write), impreso (from "imprimir," to print), dicho (from "decir," to say or to tell), abierto (from "abrir," to open), visto (from "ver," to see). Some other common verbs with regular and irregular past participles are:

despertar (to wake up)	>	despertado and despierto
invertir (to invert)	>	invertido and inverso
concluir (to conclude)	>	concluido and concluso
suspender (to suspend)	>	suspendido and suspenso
incluir (to include)	>	incluido and incluso
elegir (to elect)	>	elegido and electo

participio pasivo – m / *passive participle* The one used to form compound tenses. Examples: He comido. (I have eaten.); Fue firmado. (It was signed.) (See also: participio pasado)

partícula – f / *particle* Element used in the formation of some words. For example, "di" in "disentir" (to disagree).

partitivo – adj / *partitive* Said of a noun or numeral expressing a division of a whole into parts. For example, "medio" (half).

pasiva refleja – f / *reflexive construction* (See: voz pasiva)

perífrasis – f / *periphrasis* Verbal unity formed by a verb in a personal form and another in a nonpersonal form. Example: Sigo pensando en sus palabras. (I keep thinking about his/her words.)

período – m / *period* Group of words grammatically connected with others to complete the meaning, especially in conditional constructions. Example: Si tuviera un millón de dólares me compraría un castillo en Europa. (If I had a million dollars I would buy a castle in Europe.)

persona – f / *person* Any of the six persons in the conjugation of a verb:

Spanish	English
yo, first singular	I
tú, second singular	you (informal)
él/ella/usted, third singular	he/she/you (formal)
nosotros, first plural	we
vosotros, second plural	you (informal)
ellos/ellas/ustedes, third plural	they (formal/informal)

plagio – m / *plagiarism* Passing as one's own the writing or ideas of another person.

pleonasmo – m / *pleonasm* The use in a sentence of unnecessary words. For example, "subir arriba" (to go up upstairs), "bajar abajo" (to go down downstairs).

plural – m, adj / *plural* It is formed in Spanish by adding *s* to words ending in a vowel, and *es* for those ending in a consonant. Words ending in *z* require changing it to *c* and then adding *es*. Examples:

singular	plural
casa (house)	casas
tambor (drum)	tambores
nariz (nose)	narices

plurilingüe – adj / *plurilingual* Able to speak several languages.

poliptoton – m / *polyptoton* A figure in rhetoric in which a noun or adjective is repeated in different cases, genders, or numbers, or the same verb in different moods, tenses, and persons. Example: Ayer hablé con mi mujer, como le hablo siempre, hablándole de mis cosas pero, como de costumbre fue como si le hablara a la pared. (Yesterday I spoke to my wife, as I always speak to her, speaking about my things, but, as usual, it seemed I was speaking to the wall.) In this sentence, the same verb "hablar" (to speak) is used in the past tense of the indicative ("hablé"), in the present tense of the indicative ("hablo"), in the present participle or gerund ("hablándole"), and in the imperfect subjunctive ("hablara").

polisemia – f / *polysemy* A word that has several meanings. For example, "regla" > ruler > rule > period (menstruation).

polisílaba-o – adj / *polysyllable* (Used also as a noun.) A word that has several syllables. For example, "edificio" (building): "e-di-fi-cio," "campana" (bell): "cam-pa-na."

polisíndeton – m / *polysyndeton* The repetition

of conjunctions for rhetorical effect. Example: Y me dijo, y me volvió a decir, y no paró de hablar y de emplear un lenguaje ofensivo. (And he told me, and told me again, and didn't stop talking and using offensive language.)

por and para – **prep** / *for, by, to, etc.* With these two prepositions, it is always difficult to decide when to use one or the other. The following tips may help.

para

Used before the indirect object.

Example:

El juguete es para el niño.	The toy is for the child.

Used when referring to a place, time, cause, manner, etc.

Example:

Salieron en barco para las Bahamas.	They left on a ship for the Bahamas.

When used with "que" functioning as a conjunction.

Example:

Te di ese libro para que lo leas.	I gave you that book to read it.

por

When it precedes a verb infinitive, it can denote purpose or objective, in which case it can equal "para."

Example:

Estudio por aprender/ estudio para aprender.   I study to learn.

When preceding a noun, it is always a preposition indicating a circumstantial complement.

Example:

Camino por el parque.   I walk in (through) the park.

porque – conj / *because* "Porque" (one word) is a conjunction, and "por que" (two words) is a preposition using a relative pronoun, which can be distinguished from the other as being the equivalent of "por el/la cual/los/las cuales." Example: De la muchacha por que (por la cual) preguntas no te puedo decir nada porque nunca la conocí. (The girl about whom you asked I can't say anything because I never met her.) "Por" can also function as an adverb, as in: "por consiguiente" (consequently), or "por tanto" (therefore).

potencial simple – m / *conditional simple* (See: modo potencial) Example of the verb "estudiar" (to study) conjugated in the conditional simple:

Spanish	English
estudiaría	I would study
estudiarías	you would study
estudiaría	he/she/you would study
estudiaríamos	we would study
estudiaríais	you would study
estudiarían	they would study

Note that the various endings are added to the infinitive, as with the future tense.

potencial compuesto – m / *conditional perfect*
(See: modo potencial) It is formed with the conditional of the verb "haber" (to have, which is irregular) plus a past participle. Example of the verb "jugar" (to play) conjugated in the conditional perfect:

Spanish	**English**
habría jugado	I would have played
habrías jugado	you would have played
habría jugado	he/she/it/you would have played
habríamos jugado	we would have played
habríais jugado	you would have played
habrían jugado	they would have played

predicado – m / *predicate* What is said either affirmatively or negatively about the subject, within a construction that starts with a verb. Example: Mi hermano estudia italiano. (My brother studies Italian.) In this sentence, "mi hermano" is the subject and "estudia italiano" is the predicate.

predicado nominal – m / *nominal predicate*
The predicate that uses a substantive noun, an

adjective, a participle, an adverb, or an adverbial phrase.

Example:

using a substantive noun

Mi prima es enfermera.	My cousin is a nurse.

using an adjective

Mi amiga está contenta.	My friend is happy.

using a participle

Estamos cansados.	We are tired.

using an adverb

Mis padres fueron siempre así.	My parents were always that way.

using an adverbial phrase

Él habla a la cubana.	He speaks Cuban style.

predicado verbal – m / *verbal predicate* The predicate that uses a verb. Example: Mi primo trabaja en la ciudad. (My cousin works in the city.)

prefijo – m / *prefix* An affix placed before a word. Example: *sub*desarrollado (underdeveloped), *des*hacer (to undo). Many prefixes in Spanish are Greek or Latin. Here are a few examples of each:

Greek

*ana*tomía	anatomy
*anfi*bio	amphibious
*autó*grafo	autograph
*deca*dencia	decadence
*dia*betes	diabetes

Latin

*circun*ferencia	circumference
*equi*tativo	equitable
*extra*vagante	extravagant
*sub*terráneo	subterranean (underground)
*tri*ángulo	triangle

prenominal – **adj** / *prenominal* That which comes before a noun.

preposición – **f** / *preposition* An invariable word that introduces a subordinate clause. There are 24 prepositions in Spanish:

Spanish	**English**
a	to/at
ante	before
bajo/so	under
con	with
contra	against
de	of/from
desde	from/since
durante	during
en	in/into/on
entre	between/among
excepto/menos/salvo	except
hacia	toward
hasta	until
mediante	through, by means of
para	for/to/in order to
por	for/by/through

pro	in favor of
según	according to
sin	without
sobre	about/on/upon
tras	after

Note: Some of these prepositions can also function as adverbs, such as "según," "hasta," "entre," among others. On the other hand, some adverbs can function as prepositions, such as "salvo" (outside of, with the exception of), "excepto" (except), "menos" (less), "más" (more), "incluso" (even). Some prepositions are also used as prefixes, like "de" > "detrás" (behind), "sin" > "sinrazón" (injustice, wrong), "contra" > "contradecir" (to contradict).

pretérito anterior – m / *past perfect* It is formed with the preterit of the auxiliary verb "haber" (to have, which is irregular) plus a past participle. Example of the verb "caminar" (to walk) conjugated in the past perfect:

Spanish	**English**
hube caminado	I had walked
hubiste caminado	you had walked
hubo caminado	he/she/it had walked
hubimos caminado	we had walked
hubisteis caminado	you had walked
hubieron caminado	they had walked

Note that Spanish has two past perfects, whereas English has only one.

pretérito imperfecto – m / *imperfect* A tense that expresses a past action based more on its duration than on its completion; in other words, a continuous or habitual action with no reference to its beginning or end. In English, it can be expressed in three different ways, as follows:

Jugaba al golf.	I played golf.
	I used to play golf.
	I was playing golf.

The imperfect is formed with two different endings for *AR*-ending and *ER*-/*IR*-ending verbs, as follows:

AR	**ER/IR**
-aba	-ía
-abas	-ías
-aba	-ía
-ábamos	-íamos
-abais	-íais
-aban	-ían

Examples:

AR using "bailar" (to dance):

Antes bailaba el tango.	Before I danced/used to dance/was dancing the tango.

ER using "querer" (to love):

Él la quería mucho.	He loved her a lot, used to love her a lot/was loving her a lot.

IR using "dormir" (to sleep):

Durante las vacaciones dormíamos hasta tarde.	During our vacation we slept late/ used to sleep late/ were sleeping late.

In Spanish, the imperfect is often contrasted with the preterit, as in: Llovía cuando llegamos a casa. (It was raining when we got home.) Here, "raining" was an ongoing action when the other action took place ("llegamos a casa"). In another example, Mirábamos la televisión cuando sonó el teléfono. (We were watching television when the phone rang.), "mirábamos" is the imperfect and "sonó" the preterit.

Note: There are only three irregular imperfect verbs in Spanish: ser (to be), ir (to go), and ver (to see). Here are their forms:

Spanish	**English**
ser	**to be**
era	I was
eras	you were
era	he/she/it was/you were
éramos	we were
erais	you were
eran	they were
ir	**to go**
iba	I went
ibas	you went
iba	he/she/it/you went
íbamos	we went

ibais	you went
iban	they went
ver	**to see**
veía	I saw
veías	you saw
veía	he/she/it/you saw
veíamos	we saw
veíais	you saw
veían	they saw

There is also a "pretérito imperfecto" in the subjunctive mood. Look at the following conjugation of the regular verbs "dudar" (to doubt), "beber" (to drink), "partir" (to cut), and note that this tense has two different endings, although the first one is the most common:

dudar	**beber**	**partir**
dudara/ dudase	bebiera/ bebiese	partiera/ partiese
dudaras/ dudases	bebieras/ bebieses	partieras/ partieses
dudara/ dudase	bebiera/ bebiese	partiera/ partiese
dudáramos/ dudásemos	bebiéramos/ bebiésemos	partiéramos/ partiésemos
dudarais/ dudaseis	bebierais/ bebieseis	partierais/ partieseis
dudaran/ dudasen	bebieran/ bebiesen	partieran/ partiesen

Note also that the endings of the second and third conjugations are the same. The "pretérito imperfecto" of the subjunctive corresponds to the indicative preterit, the indicative imperfect, and the conditional simple.

pretérito indefinido – m / *preterit* Expresses a completed past action independent of the moment or time in which it is used. Example of the verb "ayudar" (to help) in the past tense:

Spanish	English
ayudé	I helped
ayudaste	you helped
ayudó	he/she/it/you helped
ayudamos	we helped
ayudasteis	you helped
ayudaron	they helped

Note: These are the endings for *AR*-ending verbs, which are different from the *ER*-/*IR*-ending verbs. The endings for the *ER*-/*IR*- verbs are the same:

comer/vivir	to eat/to live
comí/viví	I ate/lived
comiste/viviste	you ate/lived
comió/vivió	he/she/it/you ate/lived
comimos/vivimos	we ate/lived
comisteis/vivisteis	you ate/lived
comieron/vivieron	they ate/lived

pretérito perfecto – m / *present perfect* Expresses a past action taking place close to the present, as in: Han hablado con el profesor. (They have talked to the professor.), indicating that the action of speaking to the professor just happened. It is formed with the present tense of the auxiliary verb "haber" (to have, which is irregular) plus a past participle. Example of the verb "hablar" (to speak/talk) conjugated in the present perfect:

Spanish	**English**
he hablado	I have talked/ spoken
has hablado	you have talked/ spoken
ha hablado	he/she/you has/ have talked/spoken
hemos hablado	we have talked/ spoken
habéis hablado	you have talked/ spoken
han hablado	they have talked/ spoken

There is also a "pretérito perfecto" of the subjunctive mood. Its use is akin to the present perfect indicative in English, but only in subordinate clauses requiring or calling for the subjunctive, as in: Espero que Carlos haya terminado la tarea. (I hope that Carlos has finished the homework.) Conjugation of "haber" in the present subjunctive:

haya hablado	I have talked/ spoken
hayas hablado	you have talked/ spoken
haya hablado	he/she/you has/ have talked/spoken

hayamos hablado	we have talked/ spoken
hayáis hablado	you have talked/ spoken
hayan hablado	they have talked/ spoken

Sentence example: Espero que Emilia haya comido ya. (I hope [that] Emily has already eaten.)

pretérito pluscuamperfecto – m / *past perfect/pluperfect* It is formed with the imperfect tense of the auxiliary verb "haber" (to have, which is regular) plus a past participle. Example of the verb "comprar" (to buy) conjugated in the past perfect:

Spanish	**English**
había comprado	I had bought
habías comprado	you had bought
había comprado	he/she/you had bought
habíamos comprado	we had bought
habíais comprado	you had bought
habían comprado	they had bought

There is also a "pretérito pluscuamperfecto" of the subjunctive, which in Spanish corresponds to the past perfect/pluperfect, but only in sentences in which the main clause calls for the subjunctive, as in: Yo esperaba que Carlos hubiera terminado la tarea. (I hoped that Carlos had finished the homework.) In this tense, the auxiliary verb "haber" has two forms, either one being correct, although the first is the most common. Conjugation of "comprar":

hubiera/hubiese comprado	I had bought
hubieras/hubieses comprado	you had bought
hubiera/hubiese comprado	he/she/you had bought
hubiéramos/hubiésemos comprado	we had bought
hubierais/hubieseis comprado	you had bought
hubieran/hubiesen comprado	they had bought

Note: Remember that the past participle, regular or irregular, is always invariable, whereas the auxiliary verb ("haber") is fully conjugated, just like in English.

proclítica, palabra – f / *proclitic, word* Word that loses its prosodic accent when used as part of another word or group of words, as in: Te lo diré. (I will tell you.) Here, the "te" and the "lo" are proclitic words coming before the verb. If the word or words would follow the verb, then they would be enclitic words, as in: Dámelo. (Give it to me.) This is called "acento de grupo" or "group accent."

pronombre – m / *pronoun* Type of word that often functions as a noun, as in: Lo veo siempre.

(I see him/her/it always.); Ella no habla alemán. (She doesn't speak German.)

pronombre correlativo – m / *correlative pronoun* That expressing mutual relationship. In Spanish, the correlative pronouns are divided into "interrogativos" (interrogatives), "demostrativos" (demonstratives), and "relativos" (relative). Examples:

interrogativos   ask a question; they are the same as the relative pronouns but with a written accent mark. For example, "qué."

demostrativos   indicate proximity or distance of persons, animals, or things. For example, "éste" (this one), "ése" (that one).

relativos   refer to a person, animal, or thing already mentioned, called "antecedent." For example, "que" (that), "quien" (who).

pronombre cuantitativo – m / *quantitative pronoun* That which designates beings by their number without specifying (as opposed to the "numeral pronouns," which do specify). Quantitative pronouns are all used in the plural. Some of the quantitative pronouns in Spanish are: muchos (many), algunos (some), pocos (few), bastantes (enough), varios (several), todos (all), demasiados (too many), más (more), menos (less). All adjectives used with these pronouns have masculine and feminine forms, as in: Muchos son buenos. (Many are good.—referring to men); Muchas son buenas. (Many are good.—referring to women), with the exception of "bastantes," "más," and "menos." In the singular, these quantitative pronouns (as well as others used only in the singular, such as "algo" > something, "nada" > nothing), don't designate beings but just quantities with a more or less neuter meaning, as in: Han recaudado bastante dinero. (They have collected enough money.)

pronombre de complemento directo – m / *direct object pronoun*

Spanish	English
me	me
te	you
lo/la*	him/it/her/you (masculine/ feminine singular)
nos	us
os	you
los/las	them/you (masculine, feminine plural)

Examples:

direct object	**direct object pronoun**
Vemos a Juan. (We see John.)	Lo vemos. (We see him.)
Compré la camisa. (I bought the shirt.)	La compré. (I bought it.)

*In Spain it would be "le" (only for the masculine), which would apply to both persons and things, and to the direct as well as to the indirect objects.

pronombre de complemento indirecto – m / *indirect object pronoun*

Spanish	English
me	me
te	you
le	him/her
nos	us
os	you
les	them

Examples:

indirect object	indirect object pronoun
Le damos la camisa a Pedro.	Se* la damos.
We give the shirt to Pedro.	We give it to him.

*Important note: When the direct object pronouns "lo/la/los/las" are used together with the indirect object pronouns in the same sentence, the "le/les" change to "se." Example: Le damos el libro al profesor. (We give the book to the professor.); Se lo damos. (We give it to him.) Here, the "se" is the indirect object pronoun replacing the noun "profesor" (professor), and the "lo" is the direct object pronoun replacing the noun "el libro" (the book).

pronombre demostrativo – m / *demonstrative pronoun* That which substitutes for nouns. The only difference between demonstrative pronouns and demonstrative adjectives (see) is the written accent mark that is placed over the pronouns; other than that, they are identical. Today, however, the written accent mark is generally omitted.

Spanish	English
éste/ésta/esto	this one
ése/ésa/eso	that one
aquél/aquélla/aquello	that one (over there)
éstos/éstas	these ones
ésos/ésas	those ones
aquéllos/aquéllas	those ones (over there)

Notice that the singular neuter forms have no written accent mark.

Examples:

Éste es mejor.	This one is better.
Ésa es para ti.	That one is for you.
Aquél es verde.	That one (over there) is green.
Aquéllos son tuyos.	Those (over there) are yours.

pronombre indefinido – m / *indefinite pronoun*
Also called "pronombre indeterminado," it doesn't refer to any person, animal or thing in particular, like "nadie" (nobody/ no one), "nada" (nothing), "alguien" (somebody, someone).

pronombre interrogativo – m / *interrogative pronoun* Spanish interrogative pronouns are: qué (what), cuál (which, what), quién (who), cuánto (how much/how many). Note that they all use the written accent. Examples:

Spanish	English
¿Qué es eso que tienes?	What's that (that) you have?
¿Cuál te gusta más?	Which one do you like best?
¿Quién te llamó?	Who called you?
¿Cuánto pesas ahora?	How much do you weigh now?
¿Cuántos prefieres?	How many do you prefer?

pronombre numeral – m / *numeral pronoun* It designates beings through exact numbers, such as "nueve" (nine), "trescientos" (three hundred). Examples: Sólo llegaron nueve. (Only nine arrived.); Trescientos venían a caballo. (Three hundred came on horses.) With the exception of "uno" (one), all of the others are always used in the plural, and some have masculine and feminine forms (one, twenty-one, and all those from two hundred to nine hundred). There are 50 numeral pronouns in Spanish, comprising those of one word ("seven, nine"), and those of two words ("three hundred, seven hundred").

pronombre personal – m / *personal pronoun/ subject pronoun* As in English, the personal pronouns in Spanish are:

Spanish	English
yo	I
tú	you
él/ella/ello/usted	he/she/it/you

nosotros	we
vosotros	you
ellos/ellas/ustedes	they/you

The first three are singular, and the other three plural. In addressing someone in conversation, "tú" is used for the informal singular, and "usted" for the formal singular, with their respective "vosotros" and "ustedes" for the plural. The "vosotros" form is mostly used in Spain for the informal plural, whereas in other Spanish-speaking countries the "ustedes" form (the third plural) is used indistinctively for the formal and informal plural. "Ello" is the third person neuter form that can only be used in the singular (no "ellos," or "ellas," which would mean "they"), meaning that when used with adjectives or verbs acting as the subject, these would have to be in the singular too. Example of "ello": No te vas a morir por ello. (You're not going to die over it.) However, the neuter form "ello" is seldom used in Spanish.

pronombre posesivo – m / *possessive pronoun*
Replaces the noun with which it agrees in gender and number, and is usually preceded by the definite article in all four forms. Possessive pronouns are:

Spanish	**English**
el mío/los míos/la mía/ las mías	mine
el tuyo/los tuyos/la tuya/ las tuyas	yours

el suyo/los suyos/ la suya/las suyas	his/hers/yours (formal)
el nuestro/los nuestros/ la nuestra/las nuestras	ours
el vuestro/los vuestros/ la vuestra/las vuestras	yours (informal)
el suyo/los suyos/la suya/las suyas	theirs/yours (formal)

As with the possessive adjectives, since the third person singular or plural doesn't specify who the person is, the following forms may be added for clarification:

él/la/los/las/de él/ de ella/de usted/ de ellos/de ellas/ de ustedes	his/hers/yours/ theirs/yours

Examples:

Este reloj no es mío, sino tuyo.	This watch is not mine, but yours./ This watch is yours, not mine.
Esa casa no es de él, sino de ella.	That house is not his, but hers.

pronombre reflexivo – m / *reflexive pronoun*
That which is used in the conjugation of reflexive verbs: me, te, se, nos, os, se. (See: verbo reflexivo)

pronombre relativo – m / *relative pronoun* It refers to an antecedent, that is, a person, animal, or thing, already mentioned. Most frequently used relative pronouns are "que," "quien," "cual," and "cuyo."

Que	is used for both persons and things, and it means "that," "which," or "who."
Cual	is used for persons ("who, whom") and for things ("which").

Examples:

La casa que compraste.	The house (that) you bought.
La mujer que conociste.	The woman you met.
El plato que se rompió.	The dish that/ which broke.
La razón por la cual no vino.	The reason why he/she didn't come.

Quien   means "who" or "that."

Example:

Tiene que ser tu padre quien lo decida.	Your father is the one who has to decide it.

Cuyo   means "whose." As a possessive, it agrees not with its antecendent, which is the name of the possessor, but with the person or thing possessed.

Example:

Es una casa cuyo dueño es muy rico.	It is a house whose owner is very rich.

pronominal – adj / *pronominal* That which belongs or is related to a pronoun.

pronunciación – f / *pronunciation* The act or manner of pronouncing words in reference to the production of sounds.

pronunciación española – f / *Spanish pronunciation* Peculiar Spanish sounds:

The letters *b* and *v* are pronounced the same, as in "barco" (ship), "vino" (wine).

The only double consonants in Spanish are *ch, ll, rr* as in "noche" (night), "caballo" (horse), "hierro" (iron). Each one is pronounced as a single unit and can't be separated in pronunciation or in writing.

The letter *c* has two sounds, one soft and the other hard. It sounds like /s/ before *e* and *i,* and like /k/ before *a, o, u,* as in "cera" (wax), "cinco" (five), "cara" (face), "coro" (chorus), "cura" (priest).

The letter *g* has two sounds, one soft and the other harsh. It sounds like the /g/ in "goat" before *a, o, u,* as in "gato" (cat), "gota" (drop), "gusto" (taste), and as the /h/ in "he," as in "gente" (people), "gitano" (gipsy).

The letter *j* with any vowel combination always sounds like the /h/ in "hot," as in "jabón" (soap), "jerga" (jargon), "jinete" (horseman), "jota" (name of the letter *j*), "jugo" (juice).

The letter *h* is always silent, mute, in Spanish. For example, "héroe" (hero), "ahora" (now), are pronounced /éroe/, /aóra/.

The letter *q* is only used in the combinations *que* and *qui.* Examples: "queso" (cheese), "quinto" (fifth). The *u* is never pronounced.

The *ñ* is the only nasal sound in Spanish, as in "año" (year), "español" (Spanish).

Diphthongs or triphthongs are pronounced together and are never separated, unless there is an orthographical accent over the weak vowel (*i* or *u*) as in "dí-a" (day), "dú-o" (duet). Without the written accent over the weak vowel, the strong vowel always carries the main stress, as in: "c*ie*lo" (sky), "*a*ula" (classroom).

The *u* in the combinations *gue* or *gui* is only pronounced when it has a dieresis over it, as in "Camagüey" (province of Cuba), "güiro" (musical instrument).

The letter *x* has two sounds: like /ks/ before vowels, as in "éxito," and as /s/ before conso-nants, as in: "extremo" (extreme).

The letter *y* is pronounced like the *y* in "yes" when followed by a vowel, and like *i* when used by itself at the end of a word, as in "buey" (ox).

The *z* is pronounced like /s/ with all vowel combinations, except in parts of Spain, where it is pronounced like the *th* in "thin." It never has the "buzzing" sound that it has in English.

proparoxítona – adj / *proparoxytone* In Span-ish, a word that has the accent mark on the third syllable from the last. Also called "antepenúl-tima" (antepenult). Example: "húmedo" (humid), "simpático" (nice).

prosodia – f / *prosody* Part of grammar that teaches the correct pronunciation and accentua-tion of words, syllables, and letters.

prosopopeya – f / *prosopopoeia* In rhetoric, a figure by which objects or things are presented as persons, or inanimate things are presented as animated beings. Example: El árbol me habla al batirlo el viento. (The tree talks to me when battered by the wind.)

prótasis – f / *protasis* The first part of a simple or compound sentence, whose meaning is completed by the second part of the simple or compound sentence. Example: Con el tiempo todo se resuelve. (In time, all is resolved.) The second part of the simple or compound sentence is called "apodosis."

prótesis – f / *prothesis* The addition of a sound to the beginning of a word in order to facilitate its pronunciation. For example, "espina" (thorn) from the Latin "spina."

proverbio – m / *proverb* (See: refrán)

punto – m / *period (.)* Placed at the end of a completed text.

punto de articulación – m / *place-point of articulation* The articulation of Spanish consonant sounds is classified in the following groups:

bilabial (bilabial)	pronounced using both lips, like the *b* and the *p*. Example: capa (cape), cambio (change), labio (lip).
labiodental (labiodental)	pronounced applying or approaching the lower lip to the edges of the incisor upper teeth, like the *f*.

Example: fácil (easy), enfermo (sick).

interdental
(interdental)

pronounced placing the tip of the tongue between the edges of the incisor teeth, like the *z* as pronounced in Spain, or the *d* between vowels. Example: onza (ounce), rueda (wheel).

dental
(dental)

pronounced applying or approaching the tongue against the back of the incisor upper teeth, like the *t*. Example: tomar (to take), cuando (when).

alveolar
(alveolar)

pronounced by touching or approaching the upper alveoli with the tongue, like the *n* or *rr*. Example: mano (hand), perro (dog).

palatal
(palatal)

pronounced applying or approaching the back of the tongue against or near the hard palate, like the *ñ* or the *ll*. Example: español (Spanish), lluvia (rain).

velar
(velar)

pronounced with the back of the tongue touching or near the soft palate, like the *g* or the *j*. Example: manga (sleeve), jamás (never).

gutural
(guttural)

produced by the placing the back of the tongue against or

close to the soft palate, like the *c* in casa (house) or the *k* in kilómetro (kilometer).

uvular
(uvular)

pronounced with a vibration of the uvula, or with the back of the tongue in contact or near the uvula.

puntos suspensivos – m, pl / *ellipsis (…)* In writing, an omission of words at the end of a sentence or clause indicating doubt, fear, the unexpected, or the unusual of what is to follow. Example: Yo la miré, ella me miró, y después los dos… (I looked at her, she looked at me, and then we both…)

punto y aparte – m / *period, new paragraph (.)* Used when making reference to something different from the previous paragraph, or when something is considered from another perspective or point of view.

punto y coma – m / *semicolon (;)* Used to indicate a pause longer than a comma. Example: Nos fuimos al campo; llegamos cansados pero alegres después de haber dejado la agobiante ciudad. (We left for the country; we got there tired but happy after leaving the oppressing city.)

punto y seguido – m / *period, same paragraph (.)* Used to connect a concept, which, after the period, is continued or rationalized. Example: La humildad es gran virtud. Sin embargo, pocos son los que la practican. (Humility is a great virtue. However, not too many people put it into practice.)

puntuación – f / *punctuation* The system that uses various standardized marks or signs in writing to separate sentences and other expressions in order to facilitate their meaning. The punctuation marks in Spanish are:

Spanish	English
coma (,)	comma
punto y coma (;)	semicolon
dos puntos (:)	colon
punto (.)	period
puntos suspensivos (…)	ellipsis
interrogación (¿?)	question mark
admiración (¡!)	exclamation mark/point
paréntesis ( )	parenthesis
comillas (" ")	quotations
guión (-)	hyphen/dash
raya (__)	line
dieresis* (ü)	diaresis

*Only used over the letter ü, so it may be pronounced.

R

raíz verbal/radical – f / *verb root/stem* In Spanish, what is left after removing the ending of an infinitive verb. Example:

verb	ending	root
charlar	*ar*	*charl-*
temer	*er*	*tem-*
salir	*ir*	*sal-*

raya – f / *line* Used in Spanish to indicate a dialogue in writing (in English, quotation marks are used). Example:

—¿Y tú qué haces? ("And what are you doing?")

—Pues nada, trabajando como siempre. ("Well, nothing, working as usual.")

Often, it is also used in place of a parenthesis: El problema era—y era grande—que no teníamos dinero. (The problem was—and it was a big problem—that we had no money.)

Real Academia de la Lengua Española – m / *Royal Academy of the Spanish Language* Institution founded in Madrid, Spain, in 1713, entrusted with formalizing and regulating the Spanish language as it evolved, has evolved, and continues to evolve through the years. Today, its function is primarily honorary, although it is widely thought to be the most reliable source of information on the Spanish language. Between

1726 and 1739 it published its celebrated six-volume *Diccionario de Autoridades,* in 1741 its *Ortografía*, and in 1771 its *Gramática*. Its *Diccionario de la Lengua Española*—the most complete and authoritative today—is currently in its 23rd edition. Although headquartered in Madrid, the Academy has branches and academic members throughout the Spanish-speaking world.

recíproco – **adj** / *reciprocal* (See: verbo recíproco)

redacción – **f** / *editing/writing* "Redacción" refers to "editing" in the publishing world, and to "writing" elsewhere. Example: El periodista redactó el artículo. (The journalist edited the article.); Jorge redacta una carta. (George is writing a letter.)

redundancia – **f** / *redundancy* Repetition or excessive use of a word or concept. Example: Ayer te lo dije, sí, te lo dije, trata de recordar que ayer te lo dije. (Yesterday I told you, yes, I told you, try to remember that, yesterday I told you.)

refrán – **m** / *saying/proverb/maxim* Sharp and sententious saying commonly used in all languages. Examples: Al que madruga Dios le ayuda. (The early bird gets the worm.); Dime con quién andas y te diré quién eres. (You are judged by the company you keep.); Más vale pájaro en mano que cien volando. (A bird in the hand is worth two in the bush.); Más vale prevenir que tener que lamentar. (An ounce of prevention is worth a pound of cure.)

regionalismo – m / *regionalism* Word or phrase peculiar to a particular region, like in the Spanish of the Andean or Río de la Plata regions.

repetición – f / *repetition* A figure in rhetoric that consists of repeating words or concepts. Example: ¡Vete, vete ya de mi presencia, vete ya de mi vida, vete, vete! (Get out, get out of my presence, get out of my life, get out, get out!)

respiración – f / *breathing/respiration* Inhaling and exhaling air; breathing.

retórica / f / *rhetoric* The art or science dealing with the effective use of words in speaking or writing as to persuade, influence, delight, or move.

S

semántica – f / *semantics* The study of the meaning of words.

semiconsonante – f / *semiconsonant* Said of the vowel *i* or *u* at the beginning of a diphthong or triphthong. For example, "hierro" (iron), "puerta" (door), "apreciáis" (you appreciate, informal plural).

semivocal – f / *semivowel* Said of the vowel *i* or *u* at the end of a diphthong. For example, "baile" (dance), "pausa" (pause).

separación/división en sílabas – f / *separation of words into syllables* Usually done in writing, as opposed to "silabeo," which is done orally. The rules are very clear and precise in Spanish.

Rule 1   When a consonant is between vowels, it forms a syllable with the second vowel, as in: me-cá-ni-co.

Rule 2   The combinations *bl, br, cl, cr, dr, fl, fr, gl, gr, pl, pr, tr* also form a syllable with the following vowel, as in: po-bla-ción, pa-dre, re-gla-men-to, a-pre-tar, etc.

Rule 3   When two consonants are together, whether they are identical consonants or different ones (except those combinations mentioned in Rule 2), the first consonant forms a syllable with the preceding vowel, and the second consonant forms a syllable with the following vowel, as in: ob-ser-va-dor, in-mo-vi-li-dad.

Rule 4 When three consonants are together, the first two form a syllable with the preceding vowel, and the third forms a syllable with the following vowel, as in: cons-cien-te, obs-ti-na-ción.

Rule 5 When three or more consonants are combined and the last two are *bl, br, cl, cr, dr, fl, fr, gl, pr, tr,* these two form a syllable with the following vowel and the other(s) form a syllable with the preceding vowel, as in: tem-blor, in-frac-ción, sim-pli-fi-car.

Rule 6 The double consonants *ch, ll, rr* cannot be separated, as in: no-che, po-llo, ca-rro.

Rule 7 Diphthongs and triphthongs (see entry) cannot be separated in Spanish, unless the weak vowel carries a written accent mark over it, as in: dí-a, comí-ais.

Rule 8 Words cannot be separated next to the letter *x* when it is between two vowels, as in: pro-ximidad, refle-xivo. In other words, it could not be separated thus: prox-imidad, reflex-ivo. On the other hand, the *x* can be separated when it is positioned between a vowel and a consonant, as in: ex-preso, ex-traño.

ser/estar – v / *to be* Spanish has two verbs for "to be": ser and estar. Knowing when to use one or the other is a complex matter that can only be learned with practice and time. Generally speaking, "ser" is often used for permanency and "estar" for transiency, as in: Juan es bajo. (John is short.); Hoy estoy triste. (Today I am sad.) "Estar" is also often used with adjectives, especially those ending in *ado* or *ido*, such as: Estamos cansados. (We are tired.); Mis padres están dormidos. (My parents are asleep.), and with the present progressive tense, as in: Están trabajando. (They are working.) "Ser" is often used as an auxiliary verb to form the passive voice, as in: El incendio fue causado por un cigarrillo. (The fire was caused by a cigarette.)

seseo – m / The pronunciation of the sound of letter *z* and the letter *c* before *e* or *i* by using the sound of the letter *s*. This use of the *s* sound is typical of many parts of Andalusia, the Canary Islands, and most of Hispanic America, for example, "cabesa" for "cabeza," "corasón" for "corazón," "sero" for "cero," "sinco" for "cinco," and it represents a marked difference in pronunciation as compared with most of Spain.

seudo – adj / *pseudo* Used in compound words to mean "false," as in "seudohumanismo" (pseudohumanism). In today's Spanish, it is written without the Latin *p* (pseudo > seudo).

seudónimo – m / *pseudonym* Said of a writer who uses a false or ficticious name instead of his or her true one. For example, the Spanish writer and poet José Martínez Ruiz used the pseudonym "Azorín" in his literary works.

sibilante – adj / *sibilant* Said of a phoneme uttered by making a whistling fricative/affricate sound, like the Castilian *z* in "pozo" (well), "zorra" (fox).

sic – adv / *sic* Used within brackets in a quotation to call attention to the fact that such quotation, whether a word or phrase, is literal or textual.

sigla – f / *acronym* Word that is formed by the initial letters of a name or expression. Example: OEA (Organización de Estados Americanos), E.E.U.U. (Estados Unidos de Norteamérica), OTAN (Organización del Tratado del Atlántico Norte).

significado – m / *meaning* The intended meaning or sense of a word or phrase.

signo de exclamación – m / *exclamation mark/point* Spanish uses two exclamation marks, one inverted at the beginning of the exclamation and the other at the end, as in: ¡Estudia la lección! (Study the lesson!)

signo de interrogación – m / *question mark* Spanish uses two question marks, one inverted at the beginning of the question and the other at the end, as in: ¿Cómo está usted? (How are you?)

signo de puntuación – m / *punctuation mark* (See: Puntuación)

sílaba – f / *syllable* The sound of one or more letters pronounced at once or in one single utterance. There must be at least one vowel in every syllable. For example: animal (three syllables): "a-ni-mal," ferrocarril (four syllables): "fe-rro-ca-rril." A syllable is called "open" when it ends in a vowel, as the three syllables in the word "supli-ca" (he/she begs), and "closed" when it ends in a consonant, as the three syllables in the word "trans-por-tar" (to transport). Syllables of one letter are called in Spanish "monolíteras" (like *a* or *o*), "bilíteras" if they have two letters (like "ca-rri-to"), "trilíteras" with three letters (like "bondad"), and "polilíteras" with several letters (like "an-gus-tiáis," "a-griáis").

sílaba abierta – f / *open syllable* The syllable ending in a vowel, like "ca-si-ta" (little house).

sílaba acentuada – f / *stressed syllable* For example, in the word "perro," the first syllable, *pe*, is the stressed syllable. This is what is called in Spanish "acento prosódico" (see).

sílaba cerrada – f / *closed syllable* The one ending in a consonant, like "cár-cel" (jail).

sílaba inacentuada – f / *unstressed syllable* For example, in the word "campo," the second syllable, *po*, is the unstressed syllable.

silabeo – m / *syllabication* Oral division of words into syllables. For example, "caballo" > "ca-ba-llo" (horse), "motocicleta" > "mo-to-ci-cle-ta" (motorcycle). Syllabication is usually done orally.

símbolo – m / *symbol* Written or printed letter, abbreviation, mark, etc. taking the place of or standing for an object, quantity, process, etc.

silepsis – f / *syllepsis* Figure of construction consisting in not following the agreement rules regarding gender or number of words. Example: La mayoría de los invitados ("mayoría," singular noun) se marcharon. (The majority of the guests left.), instead of La mayoría de los invitados se marchó. Or, La gente llenaron la plaza. (The people filled the square.), instead of La gente llenó la plaza.

símil – m / *simile* Figure of speech consisting in comparing one thing with another as to highlight one of them and cause more effect. Example: Sus ojos son como luceros. (Her eyes are like stars.) It differs from a metaphor in that the comparison is explicit.

sinalefa – f / *synalepha* The fusion of two syllables into one in the pronunciation of vowels belonging to different words, either forming a diphthong or not, such vowels being at the end and at the beginning of two immediate words. The synalepha affects the spoken and not the written language. Examples:

written language	spoken language
fiesta especial	fies(ta es)pecial
para mi hermano	para(mi her)mano
sin tu esfuerzo	sin(tu es)fuerzo
estaba usado	esta(ba u)sado

The synalepha is key for understanding spoken Spanish, and it requires further study, as other rules apply.

síncopa – f / *syncope* Figure of speech consisting of an elision of one or more sounds within a word. For example, "Navidad" for "Natividad" (Christmas/Nativity).

sinecdoque – f / *synecdoche* In rhetoric, a figure of speech consisting in extending, limiting, or altering the meaning of words by which the whole of something is expressed by a part, or vice versa. For example, "cuarenta velas" for "cuarenta navíos" (forty sails for forty ships), "el bronce" for "el cañón" (bronze for cannon), "el pan" for "alimento" (bread for nourishment). Example of synecdoche in a sentence: Quedó sola con cinco bocas que alimentar. (She was left alone with five mouths [her children] to feed.)

sinéresis – f / *syneresis* Reduction to one syllable of vowels that are generally pronounced in different syllables. For example, "aho-go" for "a-ho-go."

singular / m, adj / *singular* Word that denotes only one, as opposed to "plural," which denotes many.

sino-si no – conj / *but* "Sino" in one word is an adversative conjunction, whereas "si no," separated, is a conditional conjunction and an adverb of negation. Example: No vale jugar la lotería si no hay suerte. (No sense in playing the lottery if there's no luck.); No es por el dinero sino por el tiempo. (It is not because of the money but because of the time.)

sinonimia – f / *synonymy* In rhetoric, a figure consisting in using synonymous interchangeable words to amplify or reinforce the expression of a concept without altering its meaning. For example, "decir," "hablar," and "expresar" are synonymous words in "Dice lo que siente," "Habla lo que siente," and "Expresa lo que siente." (He/she says what he/she feels.) Synonymy is shown also in "mujer" > "esposa" (wife), and "español" > "castellano" (Spanish).

sinónimo – m / *synonym* Word or expression with the same or similar meaning of another, like "orgulloso" > "engreído" (proud > conceited), "rebelde" > "insurgente" (rebel > insurgent).

sinopsis – f / *synopsis* Summary.

sintagma – m / *syntagma* A unit in a sequential grammatical or linguistic structure.

sintagma adjetival – m / *adjectival syntagma* A syntagma constructed around an adjective, as in "difícil de comprender" (difficult to understand).

sintagma adverbial – m / *adverbial syntagma* A syntagma constructed around an adverb, as in "cerca de mi casa" (close to my house).

sintagma nominal – m / *nominal syntagma* A syntagma constructed around a noun, as in "paisaje de primavera" (spring landscape).

sintagma preposicional – m / *prepositional syntagma* A syntagma that starts with a preposition, as in "desde mi balcón" (from my balcony).

sintagma verbal – m / *verbal syntagma* A syntagma constructed around a verb, as in "jugar al fútbol" (to play soccer).

sintaxis – f / *syntax* The part of grammar dealing with the proper connection of words in the formation of sentences, and the connection between sentences to form the period. The grammar of every language has fixed syntax rules that must be correctly followed to convey a full understanding. For example, in using the direct and indirect subject pronouns, Spanish and English differ in syntax as illustrated in this example:

Spanish	**English**
Se lo doy a Juan.	I give it to John.
syntax order:	syntax order:
IOP + DOP + V	V + DOP + IOP

Any change in that syntax order would render either sentence meaningless.

sobresdrújula – adj / (See: acentuación)

solecismo – m / *solecism* A violation of the established syntactical norms of a language. Example: Voy a por leche. (I am going to get milk.) instead of Voy por leche. Also: Ese agua no es pura. (That water is not pure.) instead of Esa agua no es pura. The word "agua" (water) takes a masculine demonstrative adjective ("ese") only to avoid the clashing of the two *a*'s in pronunciation, as in "esa agua," but the word itself is feminine, and thus the adjective has to be "pura" (pure). The same occurs with "el agua" and "la agua."

sólo-solo – adv, adj / *only-alone* One is written with an accent mark and the other one isn't. The difference is that "sólo" is an adverb, and "solo" is an adjective, as in: Sólo tengo un amigo. (I only have one friend.); Duermo solo. (I sleep alone.) Today, however, the Spanish Academy of the Language doesn't make such distinction, writing both words without an accent mark.

sonido – m / *sound* The noise made by the organs of speech or articulation.

sonora – adj / *voiced* Term applied to the manner in which a letter is pronounced by the vibration of the vocal cords. The Spanish voiced consonants are *b, v* (occlusive or fricative), *m, n, ñ, l, d, r, rr, ll, y, g* (*ga, gue, gui, go, gu*), *s*, and *z* (for example, in "rasgar" and "juzgar," that is to say, when they are positioned at the end of a syllable immediately preceding another voiced consonant). All of the five vowels in Spanish are also voiced.

sonorización – f / *sonorization* Turning a voiceless consonant into a voiced one. For example, the Latin *p* in "cepulla" to the *b* in "cebolla" (onion).

sorda – adj / *voiceless* The pronunciation of any letter without the vibration of the vocal cords, like the letters *p* and *t* in Spanish. The Spanish voiceless consonants are *p, f, z, t, s, ch, c* (*ca, co, cu*), *k, j, g* (*ge, gi*).

spanglish – m / *Spanglish (Spanish-English)*
Rather than a dialect, Spanglish is a morphological variation applying mainly to words and expressions as spoken in parts of the United States in close contact with the Hispanic population (Texas, California, Puerto Rico, New York, Chicago, etc.). For example, "carpeta" for "carpet," "furnitura" for "furniture," "celebridad" for "celebrity." It also affects the pronunciation of certain words by shifting the stress on words to the wrong syllable, like "capital" (CA-pital), "metropolitano" (ME-tropolitano), "televisión" (TE-levisión). In the areas predominatly Mexican, like Texas and Arizona, it is called "Tex-Mex." In any event, they are neither pidgin languages nor dialects in the full sense of the word.

sufijo – m / *suffix* An affix added to the end of a word, and, in particular, the pronouns that are added to a verb in order to form with it a word. For example, *ía* > "valent*ía*" (courage), *ismo* > "mecan*ismo*" (mechanism), *se* > "cansar*se*" (to get tired), *lo* > "Tóma*lo*." (Take it.)

sujeto – m / *subject* A word or group of words about which something is said before the predicate. Example: San José, la capital de Costa Rica, es muy hermosa. (San José, the capital of Costa Rica, is very beautiful.) In this sentence, "San José, la capital de Costa Rica" is the subject. The subject in a sentence can be:

a **noun**   Example: El niño estudia.
                    (The child studies.)

a **pronoun**	Example: Tú tienes que trabajar. (You must work.)
a **verb in the infinitive**, with or without article	Example: A ella le gusta bailar. (She likes to dance.)
a **whole sentence**	Example: Que vayamos a la reunión es importante. (It is important that we go to the meeting.)

The subject can be tacit or not. Example of the first case: Juan se baña por las mañanas. (John takes a bath in the morning.) Example of the second case: Se baña por las mañanas. (He takes a bath in the mornings.) In other words, the noun "Juan" is substituted with the reflexive pronoun "se."

subordinación – f / *subordination* The relationship between two sentences or clauses, one of which depends on the other. Example: Si no me pagas lo que me debes, no te hablaré más. (If you don't pay me what you owe me, I will not talk to you again.) In this example, "no te hablaré más" is the dependent sentence or clause.

subordinado – adj / *subordinate* Said of a grammatical element governed by another, like, for example, the adjective by the noun. Example: El árbol es alto. (The tree is tall.) Also, said of a sentence depending on another. (See: subordinación)

sustantivación – f / *substantivation* The forming of nouns with verbs and adjectives by the use of the definite article. Examples:

verb/adjective	noun
fumar	el fumar
comer	el comer
bello	lo bello
bueno	lo bueno

It also refers to certain verbs to which derivative suffixes are added to form nouns, like: describir > descripción, encantar > encantamiento.

sustantivo – adj, noun / *substantive/noun* (See: nombre)

T

tanto-cuanto/tan-cuan – adv / *so/so, much-as, much as* Both Spanish words lose the last syllable when immediately followed by another adverb or an adjective, as in: cuán lejos (so far), tan pronto (so soon).

terminación verbal – f / *verb ending* In Spanish, the particle that is removed from the root or stem of all regular verbs. Examples:

verb infinitive	root/stem	ending
trabajar	trabaj	ar
gerund		
cantando	cant	ando
past participle		
hablado	habl	ado
conjugated verb		
comemos	com	emos

Tex-Mex – m / *Tex-Mex* Texan-Mexican (See: Spanglish)

tiempo verbal – m / *verb tense* (See the individual entry for each tense.)

tiempo compuesto – m/ *compound tense* The one using a helping/auxiliary verb plus a past participle. In Spanish, the helping verb is "haber," and the past participle of regular verbs is formed as follows: *AR*-ending verbs, add *ado*, *ER/IR*-ending verbs, add *ido*. Examples: He trabajado. (I have worked.); Han caminado. (They have walked.) The verb "haber" is irregular in most tenses, and there are also many irregular past participles in Spanish, like "escrito" (written), "hecho" (done/made), "dicho" (said/told). These irregular past participles can also function as adjectives, in which case they agree in gender and number with the subject. The past participle in Spanish is invariable, whether it is regular or irregular. Examples:

used as a past participle	used as an adjective
He abierto la puerta.	La puerta está abierta.
(I have opened the door.)	(The door is open.)
Han escrito la carta.	La carta está escrita.
(They have written the letter.)	(The letter is written.)

tiempo simple – m / *simple tense* The one using only one verb, as in Los niños juegan. (The children play.); El perro ladra. (The dog barks.)

tilde – f / *tilde* The symbol placed over the ñ. It may also refer to the written or orthographical accent mark in Spanish.

timbre – m / *tone-pitch* Quality of sounds by which two words having the same tone and intensity are distinguished. Also, a pitch, intonation, or modulation of the voice expressing a certain feeling or meaning from the speaker. For example, "su timbre de voz" (his/her tone of voice).

título de cortesía – m / *courtesy title* The one given to a person as a sign of respect. For example: usted (you, formal singular), caballero (gentleman), dama (lady/madam), Su Señoría (Your Highness, Your Honor, addressed to a judge). Also: señor (mister, sir), señora (Mrs.), and señorita (Miss or Ms).

tonalidad – f / *tonality* (See: entonación)

tono – m / *tone* An intonation or pitch of the voice expressing a meaning or feeling. For example, "un tono despectivo" (a contemptuous/disparaging tone).

traducción – f / *translation* Literally, to render one language into another. It can be "literal," following the original text word by word, or "free," based on the meaning of the original text, but expressed freely in one's own words, like the English translation of *Don Quixote* by Thomas Shelton. Examples of literal and free translations:

literal
La casa encima de la montaña que vemos desde aquí es de piedra.
(The house on top of the mountain that we see from here is made out of stone.)

free
Me miró dulcemente con los ojos aguados, como suplicándome que le perdonara el gran daño que me había hecho.
(She looked at me with much tenderness and with tears in her eyes, hoping that I would find it in my heart to dismiss all the pain she had inflicted on me.)

transposición – m / *transposition* To make a word function as another. For example, making a noun an adjective: Los guapos no lloran. (The brave don't cry.) Here, "guapos," an adjective, is used as a noun. Another transposition would be making a verb function as a noun: El comer mucho es malo para la salud. (Eating too much is bad for your health.) Here, "comer," a verb, is used as a noun.

traslación – f / (See: enálage)

traslaticio – adj / *figurative* Word used to signify or denote something different from what is expressed in its original meaning; in other words, used metaphorically or figuratively. For example, the word "resplandeciente" (brilliant) in "una resplandeciente idea" (a brilliant idea), "soplamocos" for "bofetada" (slap/smack), or "castañazo" for "golpe" (blow).

tratamiento de cortesía – m / *form of address* For informal forms of address, the second singular and second plural are used. For formal forms of address, the third singular and third plural are required. Example:

informal sing.	**informal pl.**
¿Cómo te llamas?	¿Cómo os llamáis?
formal sing.	**formal pl.**
¿Cómo se llama?	¿Cómo se llaman?

triptongo – m / *triphthong* In Spanish, any combination of a strong vowel (*a*, *e*, *o*) between two weak vowels (*i*, *u*, and also *y*). There are eight such combinations in Spanish:

triphthong	**word**
iai	anunciáis
uai (uay)	menguáis, Uruguay
uau	guau
iei	vaciéis
uei (uey)	averiguéis, Camagüey
ieu	aliéutica or haliéutico
ioi	hioides

Note: the last two are very uncommon in Spanish.

As with diphthongs, the stress always falls on the strong vowel unless there is a written accent mark over the weak vowel, as in "venderí-ais," "cantarí-ais," which splits it into two syllables. If there is a written accent mark over the strong vowel, the syllable is not split.

trisílabo – adj / *tri-syllable* A word having three syllables. For example: mu-cha- cha (girl), ca-mi-no (road).

tropo – m / *trope* In rhetoric, the use of words figuratively; a figure of speech. The trope encompasses the synecdoche, metonymy, and metaphor.

tú-usted – pron / *you* (See: tuteo)

tuteo – m / *use of the familiar form of address* It is always indicated by the second person singular or the second person plural of all verbs conjugated in all moods and tenses. Examples: ¿Dónde vas después del trabajo? (Where are you going after work?); ¿Comisteis en casa hoy? (Did you eat home today?) Keep in mind, however, that in many Hispanic countries the third person plural is often used for both the informal and formal forms of address, meaning that the only informal form generally used in all countries is the second person singular, or "tú," from which the word "tuteo" is derived. The verb is "tutear" or "tutearse" (reciprocal). The singular polite form of address, or "usted," is constantly used in one-on-one conversations in Spanish between persons unkown to each other or deserving respect because of age, status, etc. Never are the two forms, formal and informal, mixed in the same conversation.

U

uvular – **adj** / *uvular* Sound produced by the vibration of the uvula, or the sound generated with the back of the tongue near or against the uvula, like the *j* in "jamón" (ham).

V

velar – adj / *velar* (See: punto de articulación)

verbal – adj / *verbal* Belonging to or relative to a verb; also, word by word or verbatim; also, by means of words. In speech, oral rather than written.

verbigracia – m / *example* Noun with the same meaning as "ejemplo" (example). "Por ejemplo" is an adverb meaning "for example."

verbo – m/ *verb* Expresses what the subject does with a variation of person, number, tense, and mood. The verb is part of the predicate and it is indispensable in a sentence. It must agree in number and person with the subject. When there are, in a sentence, various subjects belonging to different persons, the preferred agreement is the first person plural. Example: María y yo nos fuimos al cine. (Mary and I went to the movies.) There are cases, however, of sentences using a copulative verb, in which the subject is in the singular and the verb in the plural. Example: Esto son puras mentiras. (This is just plain lies.) Concerning a collective undetermined noun in the singular referring to persons or things, such as "gente" (people), "multitud" (crowd), etc., the verb or the adjective can be used in the singular or in the plural. Example: La gente es/son muy callada/calladas. (The people are very quiet.) In English, however, collective nouns are considered singular, as in:

The faculty of that college is unique. On the other hand, nouns having a plural form but a singular meaning take a singular verb, as in: The economics of the country is very bad.

verbo auxiliar – m / *auxiliary verb* There are basically two auxiliary verbs in Spanish, "haber" (to have), used to form compound tenses in the active voice, and "ser" (to be), used to form the passive voice. Either one requires the past participle. Examples:

active voice

| He aprendido la lección. | I have learned the lesson. |

passive voice

| El museo fue fundado hace cincuenta años. | The museum was founded fifty years ago. |

In the case of the passive voice, however, the past participle functions primarily as an adjective and must agree in gender and number with the subject, as in: El fuego fue apagado por los bomberos. (The fire was put out by the firemen.); Las casas fueron compradas por los inversionistas. (The houses were bought by the investors.)

verbo causativo – m / *causative verb* Used when the subject doesn't perform the action but causes someone else to perform it. Example: Me corté la barba en tu barbería. (I cut my beard in your barbershop.)

verbo coactivo – m / *coactive verb* The one signifying an action that requires effort. For example, "combatir" (to fight/combat), "acometer" (to attack).

verbo copulativo – m / *copulative verb* That which, together with the attribute, forms a nominal predicate of a sentence. Usually, "ser" and "estar" are the most frequently used copulative verbs in Spanish. Example: Mi amigo Rafael es carpintero. (My friend Rafael is a carpenter.) In this sentence, the nominal predicate can be found by asking the verb, "¿Qué es?" (What is it?) and the answer is "carpintero" (carpenter).

verbo defectivo – m / *defective verb* The one lacking some of its forms in conjugation, such as "abolir" (to abolish). Other defective verbs are "concernir" (to concern), "atañer" (to concern), "acontecer" (to take place, occur), and all the verbs denoting actions done by animals, such as "ladrar" (to bark), "relinchar" (to neigh), although for the most part they are used metaphorically. For example, "ladrar" in its true meaning lacks the first and second persons, but it can be used metaphorically as in saying: Yo siempre ladro cuando me levanto temprano por la mañana. (I always bark when I get up early in the morning.)

verbo deponente – m / *deponent verb* A verb with a passive form and an active meaning. Example: Los niños nacidos en Sevilla. (The children born in Seville.)

verbo frecuentativo – m / *frequentative verb* The one denoting a repetitive action. For example, "golpear" (to hit), "martillar" (to hammer).

verbo impersonal – **m** / *impersonal verb* The one making no reference to a subject. An impersonal verb is always conjugated in the third person singular of all moods and tenses, simple and compound, as well as in the infinitive and gerund. Example using the verb "haber": No hay nadie aquí. (There's no one here.) Example using the verb "hacer": Hace tres días que lo vi. (It has been three days since I saw him.) Example with the verb "llover": Llueve mucho en Cuba. (It rains a lot in Cuba.)

verbo incoativo – **m** / *inchoative verb* Expresses the beginning of an action. Example:

"amanecer" (to dawn): En el Caribe amanece muy temprano. (In the Caribbean dawn comes very early.)

"romper + infinitive": Rompió a llover. (It started to rain.)

"ponerse a + infinitive": Se puso a tocar la guitarra. (He/she started to play the guitar.)

verbo infinitivo – **m** / *infinitive verb* In Spanish, the verbs ending in *AR* (first conjugation), *ER* (second conjugation), and *IR* (third conjugation). Examples:

AR	*ER*	*IR*
cantar (to sing)	comer (to eat)	vivir (to live)

In English, infinitives are formed by placing "to" before the verb base or name, and in Spanish by the aforementioned endings.

verbo intransitivo – **m** / *intransitive verb* The one lacking a direct object, such as "nacer" (to be born), "morir" (to die). Examples: Nací en Colombia. (I was born in Colombia.); Mi abuelo murió ayer. (My grandfather died yesterday.)

verbo irregular – m / *irregular verb* (See also: verbo regular) These are verbs called "de irregularidad común" (common irregularity), that is, those affected by the same change in their conjugation. For example, if the verb is irregular in the present indicative, it would also be irregular in the present subjunctive and in the command or imperative. If it is irregular in the past or preterit, it would also be irregular in the imperfect subjunctive and sometimes in the gerund. And, if it is irregular in the future indicative, it would also be irregular in the conditional simple. Examples using "decir" (to say or tell):

first group:

present indicative	present subjunctive	command
digo (I say)	diga (that I may say)	¡diga! (say!)

second group:

preterit	imperfect subjunctive	gerund
dije (I said)	dijera (I said)	diciendo (saying)

third group:

future indicative	conditional simple
diré (I will say)	diría (I would say)

Notice that in all of the conjugations the thematic *e* of the infinitive "decir" has changed to *i*.

verbo predicativo – **m** / *predicative verb* A non-copulative verb such as "ser" (to be), "estar" (to be), "parecer" (to seem).

verbo pronominal – **m** / *pronominal verb* That which is constructed in all of its forms with an unstressed pronoun that agrees with the subject, such as reflexive verbs. Example: Voy a vestirme. (or) Me voy a vestir. (I'm going to get dressed.)

verbo recíproco – **m** / *reciprocal verb* It denotes that each of the subjects is the object of the action of the other, as in: Juan y María se aman. (John and Mary love each other.); Los amigos se abrazan. (The friends embrace each other.)

verbo reflexivo – **m** / *reflexive verb* The one in which the subject is the doer and at the same time the receiver of the action of the verb. In Spanish, the reflexive action is expressed by the use of reflexive pronouns, whereas in English it is implied rather than expressed. Example: Me lavo las manos. (I wash my hands [myself].)

In Spanish, many verbs can be reflexive or non-reflexive depending on the receiver of the action of the verb. Example:

reflexive action	non-reflexive action
Me lavo las manos.	Lavo el carro.
(I wash my hands.)	(I wash the car.)

In the first example, the subject performs and receives the action of the verb, whereas in the second, the subject performs the action that falls on the car and not on himself/herself. The reflexive pronouns in Spanish are:

me	myself
te	yourself
se	himself/herself/itself/ yourself (polite singular)
nos	ourselves
os	yourselves (familiar plural)
se	themselves/yourselves (polite plural)

Reflexive pronouns precede the conjugated verb, but they may be attached to the verb if an infinitive or present participle (gerund) is used. Examples:

conjugated verb	**infinitive**	**present participle**
Me lavo las manos.	Me voy a lavar las manos. (or) Voy a lavarme las manos.	Me estoy lavando las manos. (or) Estoy lavándome las manos.

In the case of the infinitive and the present participle, they both mean in English "I am going to wash my hands," and "I am washing my hands," respectively. Either one is correct in Spanish.

verbo regular – m / *regular verb* In Spanish, the verb that is conjugated without any variation or change in the root, stem, or ending, such as "hablar," "comer," "vivir." However, a verb can be regular in one tense and irregular in another, and even within the same tense conjugation it can be either one, or there may be an orthographical variation which in itself doesn't make the verb irregular. Examples of regular verbs in various simple tenses, using "hablar" (to speak), "comer" (to eat), "vivir" (to live) in the first person singular:

hablar:
indicative

present	**preterit**	**imperfect**
hablo	hablé	hablaba
future	**conditional**	
hablaré	hablaría	

subjunctive

present		**imperfect**
hable		hablara/
		hablase

comer:
indicative

present	**preterit**	**imperfect**
como	comí	comía
future	**conditional**	
comeré	comería	

subjunctive

present		**imperfect**
coma		comiera/
		comiese

vivir:
indicative

present	**preterit**	**imperfect**
vivo	viví	vivía
future	**conditional**	
viviré	viviría	

subjunctive
    present   **imperfect**
      viva   viviera/
                                viviese

As seen, there is no root/stem change in any of these different tense forms. Fortunately, there are far more regular than irregular verbs in Spanish (a ratio of about 80% to 20%).

verbo transitivo – m / *transitive verb* That which takes a direct object, as in: Compré un libro. (I bought a book.)—"libro" being the direct object.

verbo unipersonal – m / *impersonal verb* That which indicates natural phenomena, and is only used in the third person singular of all tenses. Example: Llueve. (It rains/it's raining.); Ha llovido. (It has rained.); Nevará. (It will snow.)

verborrea – f / *verbiage/verbosity* Excessive use of words in speech.

vernáculo – adj / *vernacular* It refers mainly to a native or domestic language of a country. For example, "el vernáculo peruano" (the Peruvian vernacular).

vicio de dicción – m / *faulty diction* The incorrect or defective use of a language.

vocabulario – m / *vocabulary* A systematic lexicon succinctly defined or explained. For example, "Vocabulario de la construcción" (Construction Vocabulary).

vocal – f / *vowel* A sound symbol graphically represented with vocalic articulation. As in English, there are five vowels in Spanish: *a, e, i, o, u.*

vocal átona – f / *unstressed vowel* Example: the second *a* in the word "Canta." (He/she sings.)

vocal tónica – f / *stressed vowel* Example: the first *a* in the word "Canta." (He/she sings.)

vocálico – adj / *vocalic* Belonging or relative to a vowel.

vocablo – m / *word* Same as "palabra."

voz – f / *voice* The sound produced by the vibration of the vocal cords. It could also mean "word" in Spanish. Example: El español tiene muchas voces latinas. (Spanish has many Latin words.)

voz activa – f / *active voice* As opposed to the "passive voice," it serves to signify that the subject of the verb is the agent and not the receiver. Example: José canta. (Joseph sings.); Los niños estudian. (The children study.)

voz pasiva – f / *passive voice* In this voice, the subject receives the action of the verb instead of being its agent, as in: *Don Quijote* fue escrito por Cervantes. (*Don Quixote* was written by Cervantes.) This kind of passive construction requires the use of the helping verb "ser" (to be), a past participle, and in many cases the preposition "por" (ser + past participle + por). The past participle, however, must agree in gender and in number with the subject, as opposed to the active voice, in which the past participle is invariable. It must be noted, however, that Spanish has a general dislike for the use of the passive voice, often using the active voice in its place, as in: Cervantes escribió *Don Quijote*. (Cervantes wrote *Don Quixote*.) In addition, the passive voice can also be expressed through the use of "se" and a verb in the third person singular or plural. In this way, El tratado fue firmado por los ministros. (The treaty was signed by the ministers.) coincides with Se firmó el tratado por los ministros. This kind of construction is called "pasiva refleja" (reflexive construction). Another example of the "pasiva refleja" is: Aquí se habla español, for El español es hablado aquí. (Spanish is spoken here.) "Se" is also used in impersonal sentences, as in: Se prohibe estacionar. (No parking allowed.); Se venden dos casas. (Two houses for sale.)

vulgarismo – m / *vulgarism* Coarse speech; also, colloquial usage of a language.

Y

y comercial – f / *ampersand* Generally, the symbol "&" is not used in Spanish, nor is there a term such as "ampersand." In some countries it is called "i commercial," in others "el signo &," and in most, simply "y" (and).

yeísmo – m / *y* **for** *ll* The pronunciation of the *ll* as *y* in many parts of Spain and Hispanic America. For example, "cabayo" for "caballo," "poyo" for "pollo," "gayina" for "gallina."

yuxtaposición – f / *juxtaposition* An absence of linking or connecting elements (such as conjunctions) in a continuous group of words. Example: La casa era de piedra, los muros de ladrillos, el techo de tejas. (The house was made of stone, the wall of bricks, the roof of tiles.)

Z

zeugma – m / *zeugma* A construction in which two or more sentences are joined by a verb (also an adjective or noun) that is mentioned only once but that is understood in the others without having to repeat it. Example: Juan es ingeniero, y también Pedro, Emilio y Ramiro. (Juan is an engineer, and Pedro, Emilo, and Ramiro also.)

SELECTED BIBLIOGRAPHY

Alarcos Llorach, Emilio, *Fonología española,* Biblioteca Románica Hispánica, Editorial Gredos, Madrid, 1974

Alfaro, Ricardo J., *Diccionario de anglicismos,* Biblioteca Románica Hispánica, Editorial Gredos, Madrid, 1964

Alonso, Martín, *Enciclopedia del idioma* (3 volumes), Aguilar, Madrid, 1958

The Cambridge Encyclopedia, edited by David Crystal, Cambridge University Press, fourth edition, 2000

Bello, Andrés, *Gramática de la lengua castellana,* Sopena Argentina, Buenos Aires, 1945

Benot, Eduardo, *Gramática inglesa y método para aprenderla,* Librería y Casa Editorial Hernando, S.A., Madrid, 1929

—*Arte de hablar: gramática filosófica de la lengua castellana,* Librería de los Sucesores de Hernando, Madrid, 1910

—*Diccionario de ideas afines,* Sopena, Argentina, 1941

Carreter, Fernando Lázaro, *Diccionario de términos filológicos,* Biblioteca Románica Hispánica, Editorial Gredos, Madrid, 1971

Casares, Julio, *Diccionario ideológico de la lengua española,* Gustavo Gili, Barcelona, 1979

Cejador y Frauca, Julio, *Tesoro de la lengua castellana,* Perlado, Páez y Compañía, Madrid, 1908

García de Diego, Vicente, *Etimologías españolas,* Aguilar, S.A., Madrid, 1964

Gili Gaya, Samuel, *Ortografía práctica,* Compendios Vox, Publicaciones y Ediciones Spes, Barcelona, 1954

—*Nociones de gramática histórica española,* Compendios Vox, Publicaciones y Ediciones Spes, Barcelona, 1955

—*Resumen práctico de gramática española,* Compendios Vox, Publicaciones y Ediciones Spes, Barcelona, 1957

Lapesa, Rafael, *Léxico e historia: palabras y diccionarios* (2 volumes), Istmo, Madrid, 1992

Marsá, Francisco, Dr., *Gramática y redacción,* de Gasso Hnos Editores, Barcelona, 1959

Martínez Amador, Emilio M., *Diccionario gramatical,* Ramón Sopena, Barcelona, 1974

Menéndez Pidal, Ramón (eds.), *Gramática histórica española,* undécima edición, Espasa Calpe, S.A., Madrid, 1962

Moliner, María, *Diccionario de uso del español* (several volumes), Editorial Gredos, Madrid, 1975

Morínigo, Marcos A., director, *Diccionario manual de americanismos,* Muchnik Editores, Buenos Aires, 1966

Navarro Tomás, T., *Manual de pronunciación española,* Hafner Publishing Company, New York, 1963

Nebrija, Antonio de, *Gramática de la lengua castellana,* Madrid, Editora Nacional, 1984

Pey, Santiago y Ruiz Calonja, Juan, *Diccionario de sinónimos, ideas afines y contrarios,* Editorial Teide, Barcelona, 1976

Real Academia Española, *Gramática de la lengua española,* Perlado Páez y Compañía, Madrid, 1908

The Oxford Spanish Dictionary, Spanish-English, English-Spanish/El Diccionario Oxford, Español-Inglés, Inglés-Español, Carol Styles Carvajal, Jane Horwood, Chief Editors, Oxford University Press, Oxford, 1996

Seco, Manuel, *Gramática esencial de la lengua española de Manuel Seco,* Espasa Calpe, Madrid, cuarta edición, 1996

—*Diccionario de dudas y dificultades de la lengua española,* Aguilar, S.A., Madrid, octava edición, 1982

Vega, Carlos B., *Diccionario universitario de términos literarios y gramaticales* (in press)

Vega, Carlos L., *Fundamentos de lengua española, gramática, fonética, fonología,* Ediciones Villamel, Cincinnati, Ohio, 1966

Vox Diccionario ilustrado de la lengua española, Menéndez Pidal, Ramón and Gili Gaya, Samuel, Editors, Bibliograf, Barcelona, 1973

Webster's New Twentieth Century Dictionary of the English Language, Unabridged, Simon and Schuster, 1979

Webster's New World Roget's A-Z Thesaurus, Michael Agnes, Editor in Chief, Wiley Publishing, Inc., 1999

INDEX

English Equivalents for Spanish Entries